Photograph by Mark Anthony Fox

# Without Reservation

# Without Reservation

Lessons from a Life in Restaurants

JEREMY KING

FOURTH ESTATE • *London*

4th Estate
An imprint of HarperCollins*Publishers*
1 London Bridge Street
London SE1 9GF

www.4thestate.co.uk

HarperCollins*Publishers*
Macken House, 39/40 Mayor Street Upper,
Dublin 1, D01 C9W8, Ireland

First published in Great Britain in 2025 by 4th Estate

1

ISBN 978-0-00-859902-7 (Hardback)
ISBN 978-0-00-859903-4 (Trade paperback)

Set in Adobe Garamond Pro by Six Red Marbles UK, Thetford, Norfolk

Printed and bound in Great Britain by CPI Group (UK) Ltd, Croydon

*To all the wonderful people I have worked with over the last fifty years in this indefinably beguiling and wonderful world of 'hospitality'.*

*Most of you have been the making of me, but even those who have exasperated, frustrated, cheated, embarrassed and bewildered me have still taught me so much about life. The vast majority of you have made that life so much better and I trust I haven't failed to acknowledge that fully – I hope you know who you are.*

*And Robert Holland, I certainly hope you do.*

*Thank you.*

# Contents

# Restaurants, life in microcosm?

In the year 2000, after more than two decades living and breathing hospitality, I was facing a dilemma. My business partner Chris Corbin and I had recently sold our first restaurant company, Caprice Holdings. Although we had enjoyed gratifying success and had been blessed with both the 'Restaurant of the 80s' Le Caprice, and the same in the 90s with The Ivy and had recently opened J. Sheekey's to similar acclaim – it no longer felt like enough. Ever since first hearing it in my twenties, I had been struck by the assertion of French writer André Gide that, 'Every man should have three careers.' His words rang in my ears now more loudly than ever, and I felt a great inner tension building. Restaurateuring was my second career (the first had been a brief foray into merchant banking). What would my third be?

For I had become bored, or thought I had, with restaurateuring. I loved the people – well, *most* of them – and enjoyed the delight they found in using our restaurants, but I feared that all the years spent incarcerated in restaurants meant I was missing out on life.

I am indebted to broadcaster Graham Norton for unwittingly gifting me a moment of great clarity about my chosen profession – or rather the profession that had chosen me. It was around this time that I heard him say that working in a bar or restaurant should be like national service. Instead of going into the army, everyone should do it. He would return to the idea in an interview with *The Times* many years later, which I'll quote from here:

'Not only do you become a nicer person to waiters in later life', said Graham, 'but also you figure out how to read people. You discover that a lot of people are vile, you discover how easy it is to be nice, how easy it is to be a shit, how easy it is to avoid being a complete shit.'

Norton talked of how you learn about teamwork, organisation, discipline, communication skills, dispute resolution and so much more. He had worked as a waiter at the Rock Garden in Covent Garden and in San Francisco in the Eighties and this clearly came from the heart.

His words resonated deeply. I saw that, rather than causing me to miss out on life, restaurants exposed me to so much of life in all its breadth. Moreover, I knew from experience the power of restaurants to transform and develop many a young person to the point of unrecognisability. I had entered the industry as a shy, reticent young adult – surprising, perhaps, when the carapace is that of a six-foot-five man – and had so benefited from my early years in restaurants. Choosing to carry on in the industry meant offering those opportunities to so many more young men and women.

I chose to stay with restaurateuring – but with a newfound appreciation of all that it gave me. It was at once a return to the familiar and yet a new beginning. I had found my 'third career'.

As I reflected further, I also understood that not only is a restaurant microcosmic of life but, through my life as a restaurateur, I have learned lessons on teamwork, organisation, discipline, and communication; I have imbibed parables, analogies, metaphors, morals and more, with oh so much still to learn and enjoy. And the more I learnt, the more confident I grew in sharing my experiences.

People underestimate the intimacy that can exist between restaurateur and guest, and how many successes, failures, heartbreaks, challenges and problems are either witnessed or shared. It was the frequency with which I found myself being confided in and embroiled in (or even refereeing) disputes, that encouraged me to start to speak my mind and dare to proffer advice. Lessons I thought were particular to my life I realised quickly were shared issues.

This book is part memoir and part lessons I have learned. A somewhat shy and introverted man has come to realise that the daunting and intimidating world of hospitality is his friend, and the more I opened my eyes to that, the richer my life would become and, in turn, hopefully that of others.

# Part 1: Starting out, Le Caprice

# What makes a great restaurant?

I have always worked on the basis that the best restaurants are created when the restaurateur makes it somewhere *they* would like to go to eat, and hope that enough other people will want to do so too. One of the reasons why restaurants fail is because the budding owner tries to people-please in its concept, second-guessing what guests are looking for rather than creating it from the heart.

You can be a restaurant owner or a restaurateur – they are very different roles. An owner runs their restaurant(s) from the boardroom, while a restaurateur does it from the floor. And the more you are on the floor, the better your restaurant. The easiest route to success is to do it the hard way.

There are many reasons why people visit a restaurant. Survey an average service as to why the customers have come and you will find myriad answers. For instance: I am with my partner, my family, my friends. It is a reunion, a celebration, a commiseration. It might be an interview, a business meeting, a seduction, a divorce or a sacking; people feel easier to do the tricky things in public because they believe there won't be a scene. How wrong they can be; I have seen some of the worst confrontations ever within a restaurant and, I must say, there is nothing more theatrical than an incident that has descended into shouting, table-tipping, or worse. It might come as a surprise how frequently great restaurants are the setting for such scenes.

Great restaurants are a catalyst for all these things – and the best restaurants are those that facilitate it. For many, restaurants come to represent 'safe places' in the ever-changing dynamics of family life. I look at the ritual of my own children having their first official outing on their second birthday with afternoon tea at The Ritz. Not that restaurants at any level are natural habitats for some children. I once surprised a telephone caller when they asked me whether it was all right to bring their children to The Wolseley.

'I don't know,' I said.

'What do you mean, you don't know?'

'Well, I don't know your children. What I will ask you to do is to imagine that you were coming to The Wolseley for a special occasion – having booked in advance, maybe even saved up for the event – and you are sat at a table next to your children. Except they are someone else's children. How would you enjoy the evening?'

'I think we'll come another time without them,' they said, laughing.

I love having children in the restaurants, but it is not so much whether *they* behave as to whether the parents do, and whether they understand that the moment they start to spoil the enjoyment of other guests then they have to act. It is amazing how quickly a child will stop crying if you take them outside. If I know the family at all, I will often offer to take a restless toddler on a tour just to give a parent a five-minute respite from holding them whilst they attempt to eat. Those five minutes can seem like hours!

I delight in finding three generations at table, and occasionally even four, especially on hearing that it was the youngest who determined the choice of venue. Children embrace a sense of occasion. I was once speaking to an actor and his family, sitting at their balcony table at The Wolseley, who told me that they were celebrating their six-year-old's birthday, and he had specified The Wolseley as where he wanted to spend it, as well as the exact table and his preferred seat.

A restaurant will often play a part in the genesis of a relationship. I still smile when I think of the heavily pregnant woman I encountered eating solo at the bar of Le Caprice. I had asked whether she was going to be comfortable enough on such a high stool in her condition. She told me, after a healthy sip of rosé Champagne, that she was actually going straight from lunch to have her baby induced and this was her last moment of freedom. 'It [her relationship with the father] all started here at the bar,' she said, 'so I thought it an appropriate place to celebrate the consequences and the next phase of my life.'

Of course, there are many types of restaurant, but I have always preferred that of the brasserie or grand café. I fell in love with these before ever stepping foot in one, thanks to my encounters with them through literature. I was drawn to Vienna by the writings of Stefan Zweig and Arthur Schnitzler – particularly Zweig's *The World of Yesterday*. At the heart of both the brasserie and the grand café is an aim to provide customers with what they need at any particular time of day. Robert Edward Norton, in his book *Secret Germany: Stefan George and His Circle*, quoted Zweig as describing the Viennese coffee house as 'an institution of a special kind – actually a sort of democratic club, open to everyone for the price of a cheap cup of coffee, where every guest can sit for hours with this little offering, to talk, write, play cards, receive post and, above all, consume an unlimited number of newspapers and journals.'

Flexibility and choice are the hallmarks of brasseries like La Coupole and Bofinger in Paris, and grand cafés such as Central and Landtmann in Vienna. When Chris Corbin and I were starting out, London, strangely, didn't have either such venues – only nominal but rather ersatz brasseries. Nowhere that people could have what they wanted, when and how they wanted it – whether it was kippers or porridge for breakfast, English tea and cakes at one table, *fruits de mer* at another, steak frites before the theatre, or a glass of Champagne and dinner afterwards.

The kind of restaurant I enjoy is the one where, as you walk through the door, there is that wave of sound and energy: the buzz of conviviality. You are warmly greeted, ideally by name, by a friendly but not over-familiar maître d'hôtel who seems to scoop you off your feet and carry you to the table. As you look around the bustling room, you adjust your hearing, noting the sound levels are neither too loud nor too muted; and on the path to your table you observe someone interesting, someone famous, a friend or two, and maybe people who really shouldn't be together at all. It all evokes a sense of belonging, and on reaching the table the refreshing realisation that no one is on their phone or taking photos and everyone is engaging with each other. You take your place and are immediately caught up with the heightened level of conversation that this sort of environment can engender. And then after the main courses someone stops mid-sentence and declares, 'This is really rather good', and someone adds, 'And so reasonably priced too.'

You feel the warm glow of being loved and included, and quickly you experience the high that makes you wish it wouldn't end.

I am not interested in temples of gastronomy where all you can hear is the tinkle of cutlery, clink of glass and the occasionally whispered 'How's yours? Would you like to try mine?' I live in fear of the hovering head waiter who knows not to interrupt but manages it with their silently intrusive presence. I want to be able to order 'the chicken' and not have it repeated back to me as '*Le poulet de Bresse avec son gilet d'épinards*, etc.' – I mean, how many chicken dishes do you have? And when said chicken arrives the head waiter whips out their instrument of fear: the Michelin 'pinkie', the little finger used to point out all the components, like artifacts in a museum. There are the three different butters to try to remember, the seven different breads and a sense that you are being judged.

I remember fondly the late, great restaurant critic Adrian (AA) Gill writing about one of these 'fifty thank you' dinners (notice how you and the staff are constantly saying 'thank you' to each other?) and asking what the Sorbets Surprise were, to which the manager chuckled condescendingly, saying, 'If I tell you then I will ruin Le Surprise!' Adrian described the quizzing of what the flavours had been as a ritual humiliation, as he struggled to identify them. It seemed strange that the restaurant didn't understand it was *their* fault he had failed. This precept applies to all businesses, not just restaurants.

Too many restaurants are chasing the money. I make it clear to my staff that if you look at a customer coming through the door as a source of income you will have a limited lifespan as a restaurant. I teach them to view that customer as an opportunity. An opportunity to give someone a great time, and if you succeed, then you will make money.

Restaurateurs tend to treat a single diner as a blight, whereas I think of them as a blessing. The manager sees a 50 per cent reduction in income, but I see them as being a 50 per cent increase, because the chances are they will leave quite quickly and the table can be used again. What's more, the single diner brings mystery, intrigue, sophistication and admiration.

I have always worked on the basis that we give people the opportunity to spend, but we don't make it mandatory. I remind staff that, often, the most interesting people in a restaurant are the least affluent – that's why they must be welcomed and cherished. They might not spend much, but they enliven the room and attract the more affluent, and the key to a successful restaurant is the mix of people.

I remember the early days of Brasserie Zédel, when I arrived to find the manager apoplectic about a single diner. The reason being that she had arrived and taken a table, ordered tap water and then only a soup, and with the first bread basket finished she was dutifully given another. She then asked for the bill.

Total: £2.25 (this was 2012 – approximately £3.40 at today's prices).

The staff were angry. I pointed out that I didn't hear anybody complaining that the table next to her was spending 'too much' with their Champagne and Dover sole. In life we must believe that everything averages out; the parsimonious woman was just as important as the Champagne-quaffers.

There is no end to the components of restaurant success, but there is no formula either. Successful restaurants defy analysis or the predictability of logarithms – they rely on and dwell in what I consider essential and yet indefinable ingredients: heart and soul.

# The birth of a restaurateur

I was born in Burnham-on-Sea, Somerset, to Charles and Molly King (née Chinn), as the youngest of two brothers, Pete being the eldest. Molly taught me zero about food other than that preparing it was a chore. The notion of finding joy in it would have been enough to set her off into a rare bout of giggling. As far as she was concerned, if it couldn't be thrown into a pressure cooker and forgotten, it wasn't worth bothering with.

My mother's cooking reached its nadir one Christmas Eve when I was ten. She declined to join us at a neighbour's party as she was 'busy' and said that no one should go into the kitchen as there were unwrapped presents in there. It was only when I returned home earlier than expected that I found out what she was up to, as I caught her just adding the last element of Christmas lunch to her hostess trolley – eighteen hours before serving. The almost-unrecognisable components

had been cooked to death by the time they went onto the trolley; they were beyond resurrection the next day.

We did occasionally go to the Queens Hotel on the seafront for Sunday lunch – a perk offered to Molly as a side benefit of her looking after the hotel's secretariat and accountancy: Melon with Ginger, Soup of the day, Paté, Tomato Juice (yes, that was a first course) or Prawn Cocktail – you get the idea. I still rather loved it, though.

And then there were, of course, all the illicit, compensatory convenience foods that Nigel Slater describes so evocatively, awakening the childhood memories of an entire generation, in his superb *Toast: The Story of a Boy's Hunger*. That picture of Nigel on the *Toast* cover could have been me at the Queens Hotel.

At the age of nine, I won a scholarship to Christ's Hospital, a boarding school in West Sussex. Founded in 1552, Christ's Hospital was a 'Bluecoat School', a school set up to offer a first-class education to those who couldn't afford it; fees were (and still are) calculated according to how much your parents could afford. The school only allowed us to wear the uniform they provided – full-length, silver-buttoned blue coat, knee breeches and mustard-yellow stockings, I will have you know! – with the admirable reasoning that should any

*With my parents and brother Pete, 1964*

child be more affluent than another this wouldn't be evident in the clothes we wore.

Here at least, as a boarder, I was afforded the opportunity to cook – maybe 'heat' would be more accurate – and the range of Vesta dishes, such as the Chow Mein (which consisted of a box of dried ingredients to be reconstituted in water) became a feature; I was even introduced to the phenomenon of risotto. I can still remember vividly the dawning realisation when I tried my first real one that rather than being reconstituted vegetables and boiled rice, a risotto was a work of art bordering on alchemy. And, of course, there was Angel Delight, which was powdered and had to be whisked into milk – instant, infallible, irresistible, but God knows what it was made of in those days.

At Christ's Hospital I always felt myself to be somewhat different to my schoolmates. Shy and self-conscious, with a propensity for blushing, I was often alone, but not unhappy with that, and I hasten to point out that being alone has nothing to do with being lonely. I played for the 1st XV rugby team, plus other sports, became House Captain and a 'Senior Grecian' (we were classic in our naming there – when I was thirteen my form name was 'Little Erasmus A'). On the face of it I

was properly achieved as a scholar, but I also enjoyed a suitable amount of brushes with authority, displaying an early indication that I would never be happy with being told what to do in life. Food made an early entry into my thinking when I argued against being punished for smoking by citing the *Encyclopedia Britannica*. I posited that because the school food was so awful I was hungry, and that according to the encyclopedia there were only three ways of assuaging this feeling: eating, taking some drug that suppresses the ghrelin (the hunger hormone), or smoking – apparently the nicotine has the same effect.

In the absence of the first two options, I argued, I was obliged to resort to smoking and therefore couldn't be punished for the school's failings.

It worked. It more than worked, as it made me think that any 'case' against me could be turned around with lateral thinking, and I have fought many a case through the courts and tribunals spurred on by this belief.

The best meals of my schooldays were those late-night ones with my fellow renegade seniors, as we conducted the clandestine ritual of 'festering' with smuggled-in beer and marmalade sandwiches.

Meanwhile, holiday jobs included being a bar-back at the Burnham-on-Sea Holimarine holiday camp. Here, my interest in the world of

Burnham-on-Sea – 'The leading light'

hospitality was piqued; and here too I had my first experience of unrequited love, after falling into a doting yearning for Val, the singer in the band. The next sally into hospitality was being put in charge of the ice-cream service at the Sea-Spray Café at the age of fifteen. The café belonged to the parents of my friend Mark Lewis. I saw how hard his parents were working to make a living, but still thought it a more exciting profession than my father's, who worked as a managing director in a 'wall and floor finishes' enterprise. I loved the interaction with customers because I had a safeguarding counter in front of me and I adored the music playing on the jukebox. My least favourite was Eric Clapton's 'Layla', but it has since stubbornly become the soundtrack of that summer in my memory. The whole summer experience of a seaside town was an incredible time of sexiness and discovery – even though I didn't fully understand the former.

Back at school, literature was starting to tell me that there was more to life, and the grander the tome, the more prevalent the eating aspect. Whilst I wasn't exactly reading *Babette's Feast*, even Hardy and Dickens were showing that delight could be had at a dining table, and the more contemporary writers revealed a connection between the prandial and sex – therefore of immediate interest. Thank you, Henry and Anaïs, for broadening the scope.

And then, in my final year at school – 1972 – we were coming to the end of a prefects' dinner when the headmaster, David Newsome, said, 'Let's all go back to my study and warm a bottle of claret in front of the fire.' This felt like I had morphed into literature, and was the first time I understood that wine was a creation rather than just a means of intoxication. I was ready and voracious to learn more. The cork removal was a different form of popping the cherry, but almost as carnal. I think of it today as my Rosebud moment – when life seemed innocent and carefree.

Solitude has always been a comfort to me. When we finished our A Levels, all my fellow 'Grecians' and I were allowed to exeat for the day until late. Instead of rushing off in one of the packs heading to London for debauchery at the Marquee Club, I took the train to Petworth to have lunch at the Petworth House Hotel, and then visited the house itself to see the legendary collection of J. M. W. Turner paintings that the artist produced there, thanks to the patronage and friendship of the owner, Lord Egremont. And therein was the genesis of my fascination with patronage and the notion of nurturing artists and writers.

As for the meal, I can still remember the rollmop herring and *Truite aux amandes* I ate at lunch. Sadly, the hotel seems to have disappeared, but my love of solo dining has endured.

It was arriving in London at the end of 1972, aged eighteen, that was the real catalyst for my interest in restaurants.

After graduating from Christ's Hospital, I decided to forego university and take a job in banking with Kleinwort Benson. The truth was, I had no clear-cut idea what I wanted to achieve with my life. Christ's Hospital had afforded me inspiration and access and choice in the form of music, literature, theatre and architecture, and I had plenty of aspirations in the arts, but I was questioning my ability to be a success in any of those fields. I wanted to be an architect but just knew that I wasn't talented enough and I had to find something else.

During my time working in the City I read Luke Rhinehart's novel *The Dice Man,* which tells the story of a bored psychiatrist who makes decisions about his day-to-day life based on throwing a die. The book took a hold of my imagination, so much so that I started to make decisions in my own life on the throw of the dice. It might be where to eat, which bar to go to or what to wear. And then, the more the bank bored me, the more the dice-throwing played a part. I would have morning decisions to determine who I was that day or how I behaved. Would I be a film star or maybe Long John Silver? My colleagues could never work out why I limped around the office squawking 'Pieces of Eight' followed by a slap to the shoulder and a muttered 'shiver me timbers'. I was evidently really bored.

I would also gamble extensively – a bug I had caught quite seriously having received a tip for the 1973 Epsom Derby; after backing eventual winner Morston at 33/1, I was hooked. Every Friday lunchtime I would challenge myself to place every penny I had on horses, and if at closing time I hadn't won anything, there was no money for the weekend. There were no ATMs in those days.

(I learned in time that a true gambler, rather than a 'better', needs to have real risk involved, otherwise the joy of winning is numbed. Lucian Freud explained this many years later – that losing to the gangster Kray brothers and having to hide, borrowing to bet with no prospect of repaying if failing, or using Great Train Robbery proceeds that criminals asked him to safeguard were all part of the thrill of gambling. Once success meant he could afford to lose the bet, the pursuit lost its allure.)

When I had the money, and the dice decreed it, I ate out. My first port of call in this history was Italian restaurants. I was catching the tail end of gingham tablecloths, candles in wicker Chianti bottles, mural views from the Bay of Naples restaurants, but more importantly the emerging legacy of Mario Cassandro and Franco Lagattolla, whose Soho trattoria La Terrazza was filled with the 'Swinging London' crowd. You need look no further than Alasdair Scott Sutherland's book *The Spaghetti Tree* to realise how wide was their influence and how their growing empire and the subsequent success of their former colleagues, such as Alvaro Maccioni – who went on to open the eponymous 'Alvaro' and subsequently the ground-breaking Club dell' Aretusa, on the King's Road in Chelsea – were fundamental to a culinary revolution.

The likes of La Famiglia, San Frediano and Meridiano inspired me for many reasons. These quintessentially Sixties' restaurants were at the heart of the breaking-down of the all-prevalent class structure, and soon we were seeing royalty (Princess Margaret and Lord Snowdon in particular) sitting down with celebrated East End photographers such as Terence Donovan and David Bailey, or indeed fellow photographer Lord Litchfield, as well as actors, pop stars and models, and then every combination of every demographic in between. It chimed with my deep-rooted love of egalitarianism, fomented for me at my melting pot of a school, and I started to understand the role of design as exemplified by the 'Pop' modernism of Pizza Express that had been developed by the inimitable Enzo Apicella, the designer, cartoonist and restaurateur who was also responsible for the look of all of the aforementioned Italian restaurants in Britain.

This is what stimulated my latent interest in restaurants, and even my twenty-first birthday lunch at the Spanish Salvadors El Bodegón in Park Walk showed me so much about the greatness of the continent. It was about that time that I experienced my first proper foreign holiday, and even grilled fish on a Greek island was revelatory.

There were other innovations to observe and absorb, such as the Golden Duck in Hollywood Road, the Conran/Carluccio Neal Street Restaurant, and then on to La Croisette and Le Suquet, Pierre Martin's revolutionary fish and crustacea restaurants, not forgetting probably the most important early influence of Barbara Hulanicki's mind-blowing Rainbow Room at Biba, in the early Seventies. This was the first time London had really seen contemporary glamour since the pre-war days of the Embassy Club and Café de Paris.

I had found a passion, and it certainly wasn't banking. Could it possibly morph into a career?

# Rolling the dice

I understood very quickly that I had made a big mistake by joining the bank, so I remedied the error by applying to and securing a place at Cambridge University. Relief for my parents, because they really felt that it was unusual for a 'Prime Minister in waiting', as they would have me, not to have a degree. With a clear path ahead of me now, I only needed to decide what to do in the interim ten months before the new academic year began. I was supplementing my earnings at the bank with a part-time job in a Chelsea wine bar called Charco's, and I decided to make that a full-time job.

Charco's was an early pioneer of the wine bar phenomenon of the 1970s, which came about because of a cartel maintained by all the pubs preventing the granting of new 'full licences' – and only limited wine bar licences. It was owned by the caterer to the Royal Family, Searcys, and was a sister operation to the larger and more licentious 'The Loose Box'.

I found I was comfortable in my barman role at Charco's and was soon promoted to assistant general manager – and what with living and working on the King's Road in the early Seventies, I was coming out of my shell.

When my university matriculation papers came through, this prompted more indecision, followed closely by uncertainty.

It was time to roll the dice.

The matriculation dice throw was so important that I used two dice. It is fair to say that the majority were all assuming I would take up the place, albeit at a changed time and with a very different agenda. 'Two sixes' would dictate that if I achieved a managership of Charco's or a similar bar within a month of turning twenty-one, I would skip university altogether and make my career in hospitality.

The double-six option was highly unlikely to win because it was quali-fied by other circumstances, but it needed to be there to satisfy my own Dice Man risk rules. And then it came up and I was both exhilarated and nervous, but also realised that I had a dilemma because I couldn't wait for the qualifying element to transpire as I had to return my papers. This was soon remedied by the owners of Charco's calling me in to be advised that I was indeed going to be the manager. 'The die was cast.'

And so I made the foolish mistake of foregoing my place at Cam-bridge. This is something I have regretted all my life. It was perhaps my first major life lesson, so please learn from me and don't ever abandon yourself to the whims of chance.

Within two years of being frustrated by Searcys refusal to invest in the fabric of the space that I now managed, I succumbed to an offer to join the burgeoning mini-empire being established in Battersea by a French restaurateur called Jean-Michel Gautier. His businesses included a restaurant, wine bar, patisserie and wine importer, and I learned my trade there as assistant director. But it was an unhappy time that often found me enviously checking out the movement of my colleagues as I floundered within the constraints of a job that was strangling me.

And so I started the quest for how my life should develop. The nadir of my search was reached when I found myself in front of the principal of a careers guidance agency, having taken their facile test.

'What can we do for you, Mr King?'

'I am lost in the search for a vocation. I feel I can do anything, but I crave the direction and help of someone who can tell me unequivocally what I should do with my life.'

'We get asked for this all the time, and while normally it is deemed impossible to answer, in your case we can say unequivocally what we feel is the career for you.' *Drumroll and bated breath.* 'Unquestionably you should be an accountant.'

I know why they opined this, because I am inherently mathematical and logical, but it was the last thing I wanted to hear.

'The only branch of accountancy I could possibly countenance would be turf accountancy.'

At this he got excited, saying that would answer the more flamboyant aspect of my character, which he couldn't put his finger on. This would be perfect.

I left.

Everybody had advice, and the people-pleaser in me went into overdrive trying to accommodate the perceived wishes of my family, my friends, my peers – the only person excluded was myself.

I only achieved focus through two parental interventions. The first was when I dragged myself back home to Somerset at the behest of my father because the owner of the company that he ran, Pyrok – a rather mundane creator of protective coatings for buildings – had asked whether I would like to become my father's successor. I felt I was obliged to fulfil this wish, and I can still remember the anguish I experienced on the train as I travelled to ratify it. But, more particularly, I still see the tears of joy running down my father's cheeks when I finally plucked up the courage to say 'no' just before the final interview. He had concealed that he really didn't want me to join him but felt obliged to support the request. He was clearly the source of my 'people-pleasing'. He later told me, on retirement, that throughout his time with Pyrok there hadn't been a day when he hadn't dreaded going to work. This steeled me to be more selfish in the pursuit of a career, a resolve that was further strengthened when my relieved mother said, 'I know I always talk about you being Prime Minister, but all I really want for you is that you don't wake up aged thirty and start regretting.'

But I owe the decisive intervention of my career to John Maxwell, or Max, the brilliant front-of-house manager for the hottest new restaurant in town at the time, Joe Allen. I met Max as a customer at Joe Allen, and as he lived in Battersea we started to see each other more. Max had a first-class degree from Harvard and was a Rhodes Scholar, and yet was happy working in restaurants. One day I mentioned to Max that I wanted to get out of the industry and he advised me not to. He asked me what I liked about the business and then told me, 'You're going to come and work at Joe Allen.'

I said, 'I can't do that, I'm an uptight Englishman.'

Under Richard Polo (surprisingly an ex-accountant and US naval man), Joe Allen was like a speakeasy in feel and attracted all the theatre world and actual royalty.

He said, 'No, no, no. You're going to come and work here and we'll teach you how to run a good restaurant. And more importantly – and I think you'll get much more out of this – we're going to teach you how *not* to run a good restaurant.' And that is what I did.

# An early lesson in ramifications

Up until well into the Nineties, the piano that stood near the entrance to Joe Allen bore two deep dents in its lid. These had been instrumental in a significant lesson I learned early in my career.

When I joined the staff in 1979 there was a lot to take on board, but the two years that followed would prove to be among the most formative of my career. One immediate challenge I faced was my relationship with the general manager, Richard Polo. Richard didn't seem to like me and was, I realised in retrospect, intimidated and threatened by my presence. He behaved terribly, readily assigning me menial tasks and often trying to humiliate me – maybe in an attempt to get rid of me. He nearly succeeded, but once I learned that if I didn't allow anything he said to get to me, and always cheerfully acceded to requests and orders (rather than begrudgingly and sulkily trudging off to complete them), his bullying lost its power. To Richard's credit he saw this too and changed tack, and as a consequence we became enduring and close friends for over forty years.

But that's not the point of this story, which comes instead from one of his admonishments. It was a Saturday night in the summer of 1980 and we were serving theatregoers who were in their 'dinner break' of an all-day performance of *Nicholas Nickleby* at the Aldwych Theatre. The production was eight and a half hours long and there wasn't too long a break between the two acts.

A table of four called me over to ask where their food was and were clearly quite agitated. Now, the maîtres d'hôtel didn't get involved in service, but on this occasion I felt it necessary. Head chef Martin Wilson, on the range, was surprised to see me in the kitchen and even more so when I asked him, 'How soon for Table 31?'

'Don't ask,' came the reply.

'I just did,' was mine.

'I said don't ask!'

'Well, I have to ask, because unless I give them an answer they are going to leave.'

'I SAID DON'T FUCKING ASK!! FUCK OFF!!'

'OK, I won't ask – I'll check myself.' And I looked around the front of the 'pass' to see that Table 31's food was actually next up. 'Ah, next up – thank you.' And went off to inform them. Having done so, I was just telling my colleague Tim at the desk what a complete dickhead Martin was and why couldn't he have just told me rather than do this power play, when my colleague's eyes flared wide. He blanched and shouted, 'Turn around!!'

I did, to see Martin racing up between the tables brandishing a big cleaver, which he clearly intended to bury in my skull. Tim tried to intercede and I side-stepped to avoid the blow, but in truth I feel that even psychotic Martin was aware that murder was not suitable retribution. He dissipated some of his fury by slamming the handle down on the piano lid twice, leaving the indentations, before the chefs hauled him back to the kitchen.

Later, Richard Polo arrived and took me outside – I assumed to apologise for Martin's egregious behaviour. But I was quickly disabused of that notion; it was me Richard was furious with, not Martin.

He explained that I should indeed have 'fucked off' out of the kitchen when told to, rather than aggravate a clearly stressed Martin even more.

'But what about the table?' I indignantly asked.

'You should have sacrificed it; apologised and picked up their bill,' he said.

I didn't understand until he explained that I had risked Martin completely going berserk and either walking out or been rendered useless for the rest of the evening service, thus jeopardising the 300-odd covers expected. If that had come to pass, all 300 would have had a terrible time rather than just one table. For someone who is good at gambling, I had failed to play the odds – but I had certainly learned a great lesson.

# Peter Langan

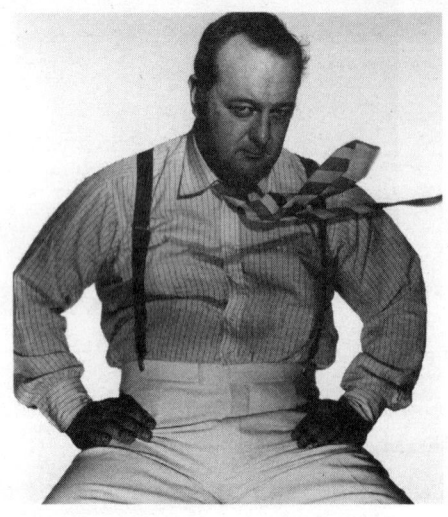

First among my restaurant heroes has to be the late, great Peter Langan, the wild Irishman who started life in the oil trade and then became a chef. After opening Odin's and Odin's Bistro in the late Sixties he went into business with the actor Michael Caine and chef Richard Shepherd to open Langan's Brasserie, in Stratton Street, off Piccadilly, in 1976.

Peter wins my accolade for his vision, his uncanny eye for detail, innate feel and understanding as to what makes a great restaurant. But while he is my hero, I certainly did not see him as a role model.

On the contrary. Peter was a compulsive drunk capable of falling asleep on the floor, having asked a series of female customers whether they were wearing stockings or tights, or trying to bite their ankles. He exasperated Michael Caine by, for instance, being chased out of Ma Maison in Hollywood for urinating in a restaurant pot plant at a time when Caine was trying to help him launch a restaurant there, or indeed

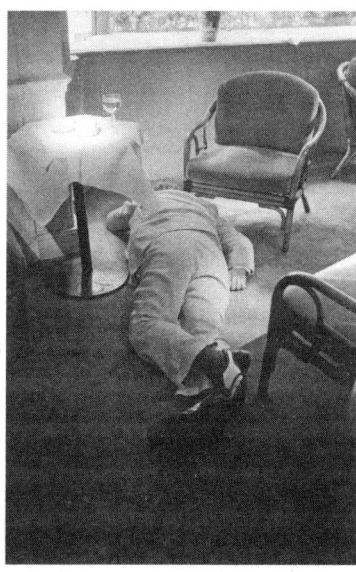

being intolerably rude to the Hollywood stars that he brought to Stratton Street.

He was indubitably incorrigible and indefensible – but I loved him. He was the man who helped me appreciate the impact of original art in restaurants. The walls of Langan's were hung with works by the likes of Lucian Freud, Patrick Procktor and David Hockney, who also illustrated the menu. As an up-and-coming artist, he and others had given paintings in lieu of meals at Peter's previous restaurant, Odin's. He was the man who taught me that the secret to good lighting was shadow. And I loved that he was an egalitarian – the man who, when creating Langan's Brasserie, said, 'I want a place where a taxi driver can sit down with a duchess.'

For me, Langan's Brasserie was the apotheosis of what a restaurant could be. Mysterious, surprising, exciting, sexy and uniquely capable of transporting those lucky enough to land a reservation into a world that previously felt privileged and unattainable. Populated by actors, rock stars and royalty, where Dudley Moore was dubbed the 'house pianist' and celebrity photographer Richard Young captured all their comings and goings in the tabloids and magazines. And yet it was where I realised that the most fascinating people in a great restaurant were not necessarily the richest.

It was at Langan's, in what must have been 1977, that I first met Chris Corbin and sealed a relationship that was to become a lifelong friendship and business partnership. Chris and I were both slightly taciturn individuals but found in each other kindred spirits. I liked the fact that he was real and sincere. When we met, Chris was one of the managers at Langan's, working under the general manager, Andrew Leeman. Andrew taught us all a great deal about hospitality, and whilst Chris and I never inherited his chaotic hedonism he sure knew how to look after people – though he did once turn Mick Jagger away from Langan's because he was wearing jeans. My favourite story about Andrew was that it was his account to John Cleese of finding a dead body at the Savoy when a trainee that led to the *Fawlty Towers* classic episode 'The Kipper and the Corpse'. In many ways Andrew pioneered the new phenomenon of the 'personality maître d'hôtel' with his charm, good looks and suavity. 'He strode through the restaurant like a Greek God,' was Fay Maschler's verdict. We lost Andrew, too young, in 2007.

My career was shaped by Peter in other ways, too. Towards the end of 1979, Peter walked through the door of Joe Allen late and looked me in the eye. 'They tell me you should open my next restaurant,' he said.

What?

I was only twenty-five and surely not experienced enough, but he was determined, and that set us off on a quest to find the perfect location to create our dream – well, *his* dream – under the working title 'Joe Langan's'. And although the restaurant would never come into existence, that name embodied what Chris and I set out to do ourselves two years later when we took the vacant 'Arlington Restaurant' on Arlington Street – a combination of Joe Allen and Langan's. And I was always underpinned by that little extra belief that Peter gave me, which he still does to this day.

I still giggle when I recall sitting in the bar with Peter at Langan's, where we were joined by his assistant at the time, Beth Coventry. Beth is the sister of London's then most eminent restaurant critic, Fay Maschler. She went on to be a highly respected chef and is still proprietress of Hampstead's gastropub The Wells. Beth joined us with some urgent correspondence, having struggled to catch Peter sober. He tended not to get so drunk when with me, so she grasped the opportunity and offered up a particularly vituperative letter of complaint with two foolscap pages of carefully laid out green-ink anger. Beth and I awaited the inevitable outburst, and yet it wasn't forthcoming – Peter just asked for a pen and, grasping it in a childlike manner, he articulated as he wrote:

'"Execrable" has three Es and "Inedible" only two.'

How I envied him in that brevity, but of course, as with most of his breathtaking and candid actions, there was never going to be a chance to emulate this. He was confronted with another complaint one day in person, by a very grand, dowager-like lady who had come down from the 'powder rooms' and thrust a dead cockroach in front of Peter's face. 'What do you call that, Mr Langan? – you should be ashamed.'

Peter took the large cockroach delicately between his index finger and thumb, just as it had been presented, and having inspected the cockroach carefully he popped it into his mouth exclaiming, 'That's a cockroach', then ostentatiously swallowed it, adding, 'Delicious.'

He adhered to the Machiavellian maxim: 'It is better to act and repent than not act and regret.' Much of what he did was staged for effect, but often he was out of control because of the drink. To put the drinking in perspective, it usually continued until closer to breakfast, and yet he still managed to get up of a morning promptly.

I remember collecting him from his Wimpole Street flat one morning to take him to Bath to attend the opening of a new Chicago Pizza Pie Factory created by Bob Payton. Peter staggered out of the door after an unexpectedly short wait on my part, clutching two wine glasses and a bottle of red wine: *'Le Beaujolais Nouveau est arrivé!'* he shouted,

*Robert Marchant* – Peter Langan's Feast for David Hockney at Glyndebourne.
*Note Peter Langan on far left, without coat and his back turned . . .*

adding '*Et moi aussi!*' After a long day I got him back to London in pretty good shape, which is more than could be said for David Hockney and friends after their day with Peter at Glyndebourne.

The occasion was the first night of Stravinsky's *The Rake's Progress*, designed by David Hockney. Peter was determined to do Hockney proud, and in the tradition of Glyndebourne had provided an extraordinary spread for the interval supper. As you can see captured in Robert Marchant's painting *Peter Langan's Feast for David Hockney at Glyndebourne,* a Bacchanalian feast lay in store, but in true Langan style it was made more memorable by Peter collapsing over the trestle table and crashing it to the ground before anything could be eaten. Normally the likes of Peter Langan are anathema to me, but there was no one quite like him, and I loved him.

Chris and I treasure a particular moment from the 1990s, some years after Peter's death. On a snowy and icy day I returned to Le Caprice at the end of lunch and came across Chris attending to a clearly upset Lady Pamela Harlech, the London editor of US *Vogue*. She had slipped and fallen outside and was both shocked and injured, with grazes down her leg and even her famous helmet of rock-solid hair slightly dishevelled. As Chris tried to calm her she fretted as to what she was going to do, as she was due at a very important meeting and couldn't possibly attend laddered and bloody.

'Don't worry,' said Chris, 'we have spare hosiery for this very reason.' He started to turn away and then paused, hesitating. I saw the beginning of a strange smile on his face, which broadened as he turned back to face us. I knew what he was going to say, and attempted to stifle incipient laughter, which in turn set him off until, barely able to get out the words, he said, in a slightly Irish brogue, 'Are you wearing stockings or tights?'

Peter's catchphrase. Neither of us ever thought we would have the occasion to ask that question.

Lady Harlech watched on perplexed as Chris and I doubled up in hysterics, before catching on to the allusion and joining in. She knew and had suffered at the hands of Peter herself.

When I think of all of my regrets in life, one that comes readily to mind is losing Peter Langan's tie.

Let me explain 'The Tie'. One morning, shortly before lunch service, into Le Caprice saunters – no, staggers – Peter, who struggles onto a bar stool for a glass of Champagne. Chris and I knew that this spelled trouble and had learned that the only way to prevent him wreaking havoc was to get him back out through the door and distract him elsewhere. Peter was in his uniform of white linen suit, sporting a beautiful yellow polka-dot tie, which elicited a compliment from me.

'You like it? Then it's yours,' he pronounced and started to untie it.

'But it is not yours to give away,' I said.

'What do you mean? Of course it's mine!'

I insisted it couldn't be his tie, as it was too clean – no stains.

He laughed and explained that was because he had just been into Turnbull & Asser to buy a replacement for the one that he had managed to lose overnight. As he gave me the tie he said portentously, 'Look after it and remember me.' Now the 'remember me' was hardly in the 'Dido's Lament' category, but it was poignant enough, and when he died not that long afterwards, in 1988, it haunted me. That tie became one of my treasured possessions and played its part in some of the most important decisions of my life. When I had difficult situations and confrontations in the day ahead, I would wear that tie and it was as if it gave me a surge of confidence.

And then one day I received a call from our dry cleaners.

They explained that a driver had made the cardinal error of leaving the clothes collected for cleaning in the van overnight and everything had been stolen, including mine. They just wanted to verify the contents: 'Three suits, eight shirts – all bespoke.' I wasn't concerned about the suits, as insurance would cover replacements. 'And a tie – is that it?'

Oh no. Not the tie. Ironically, Peter's tie was only with them because of a tiny spot of wine, which would have made Peter laugh mockingly – but that spot had felt as ominous as the drops of wine falling on the bride's dress in the movie *The Deer Hunter*, signifying bad luck. The proprietor couldn't understand my obsession with the tie in the face of the much bigger loss of the suits. I wanted to cry.

It was irreplaceable (I discovered that the design was discontinued at Turnbull's). I miss that tie to this day, as indeed I do its previous owner. I yearn for its support.

# Partnership

Chris and I got to know each other better after I joined Joe Allen in 1979, when we frequented each other's restaurants, often meeting after service, too, or to go out lunching at places that offered adventure and discovery to our still-inexperienced palates: restaurants in Chinatown, Greek tavernas in Soho or the Kosher Luncheon Club in Whitechapel. More often than not we were joined by Liam Carson, another manager at Langan's, who I am afraid I usurped in forming a bond with Chris in terms of forging a future together.

Liam went off on a more exciting and wild journey with manager-ships of the Kensington Roof Gardens, Maunkberry's Club and particularly the Groucho Club, which was both his triumph and down-fall. There were too many temptations, and although he made the Groucho's reputation and its success, it came at a price. When his

patient wife Gabby extracted him from the danger that the club had become, they went to live in France, but that was not the life for Liam and on returning to London he never enjoyed the success or glamour that he had before. Sadly Liam, who was the same age as me, died at the age of fifty-one, and it was particularly poignant that when I was leaving the funeral I saw John Spiteri, veteran maître d'hôtel of many a successful restaurant (St John, The French House, Sessions Arts Club, et al) and asked him whether he would like a lift back to Liam's wake at the Groucho he pertinently and wisely said, 'No thanks – I don't believe in returning to the scene of the crime.' Sadly apt.

Chris and I were discovering that we had similar tastes, ambitions and aspirations and resolved to open a restaurant together. As we searched for the appropriate site, cognisant of our budgetary limitations, Chris was approached by fashion magnate Joseph Ettedgui, founder of the Joseph stores, who wished to emulate the success of fashion house restaurants in Paris. His offer to finance a restaurant was met by Chris saying that he would be interested, but only if it was with Jeremy King.

I knew Joseph from my time working at Charco's wine bar in Chelsea in the early Seventies, when he was making the transition from hairdresser to fashion retailer, opening the first shop beneath his hairdressers, Salon 33, on the King's Road. It was a big success thanks in part to his association with the emerging designer Kenzō Takada, founder of the Kenzo brand.

It seemed too good to be true, but we proceeded and soon found available the short-lived and recently failed restaurant 'The Arlington' on Arlington Street – the site of the old Caprice, the great post-war haunt of the world of showbiz, film and fashion that had closed in 1975. The restaurant had originally come about after a falling out in 1945 between The Ivy owner Mr Abel (Abel Giandolini) and his maître d'hôtel Mario Gallati. Gallati left The Ivy to set up Caprice, which came to represent 'showbiz', whereas The Ivy was about theatre. It seemed natural to return to the old name, although we had to slightly change it (to Le Caprice from Caprice) for trademark reasons. (The irony, of course, is that when re-launching the restaurant again some forty years later, I reverted to the name Arlington, for similar reasons.)

The plan was for Joseph to handle the design, while Chris and I would get the restaurant open and operating. Modernist architect Eva Jiřičná was hired and we set about transforming a dusty brown edifice into a mono-chromatic gleaming tribute to a new modernism – all for £30k, which was a steal, even at the time. (When we eventually opened, the remaining Caprice customers from before its closure in 1975 were not impressed to find the ruched pink silk had gone, replaced by monochrome.)

The path to launching the business was a rollercoaster of problems and emotions, with no way of knowing whether we were about to change the face of restaurateuring in London for the Eighties or crash in flames. I think the 'trade' was fascinated and happy to predict the latter. It was a lonely, vulnerable time for us, so we particularly appreciated a supportive site visit from American restaurateur and friend Bob Payton.

In the Seventies Bob had opened a series of American-style restau-rants, notably the Chicago Pizza Pie Factory, Rib Shacks and Henry J Bean's on the King's Road. He walked in one morning, just as the builders were constructing (re-constructing) the rickety but effective lighting pelmet. He was effusive and enthusiastic, and asked for our telephone number. I realised I had no paper, so I picked up a piece of wood – a pelmet offcut – and I used it as a 'card'. Shortly before we opened the restaurant he sent it back, with one side in brass and these words engraved:

*Chris & Jeremy*
*Best of Luck*
*Leave some for me*
*Bob Payton 493 9316*

We were going to need that luck . . . but I treasured that gesture and still have the plaque on my desk – for many reasons, but not least because Bob was ripped away by an untimely death when his car

overturned on the motorway in 1994. I would urge everyone to always grasp the chance to create a memory.

The opening of Le Caprice in September 1981 went wrong – spectacularly so – and we were soon at loggerheads with Joseph and his brother Franklin over how the restaurant should be run. We reached such an impasse that just four months later we were forced to close. While this felt catastrophic at the time, in truth and in retrospect it was the best thing that could have happened to us. (And in subsequent years my relationship with Joseph would mend, in large part due to the intervention of his wise and wonderful wife Isabel, so that by the time he left us in 2010 I was privileged to be considered a close friend.)

The closure happened on the eve of my first marriage, to the arts producer Debra Hauer, in San Francisco on 8 January 1982. I remember arriving in California to receive a phone call from Chris telling me that Joseph's lawyers were demanding we buy the brothers out within two weeks and in the meantime not pay any bills. We were therefore trading insolvently, and I told Chris that unless we could show within twenty-four hours that we had a credible buyer we would have to close immediately.

My first port of call was Bob Payton, but we couldn't act quickly enough and I had to field a phone call at breakfast that day in front of all of Debra's close family. As I listened to Chris confirm the closure I had to pretend it was all only good news – I had to keep it secret in order to avoid ruining the wedding. Debra and I promptly cancelled the honeymoon and were soon back in London. I had to try to turn disaster into positivity.

Chris and I met on my return and he told me that he had already secured employment elsewhere. A career-determining conversation ensued. I told him that we had to give it another try; that we would regret it for the rest of our lives if we didn't. And if we attempted to 'phoenix' the place and failed nobody would think worse of us and at least we would have no regrets, but if we managed to make Le Caprice work against the odds then 'we would be the toast of London'. I am still uncomfortable with that phrase, but it galvanised us both to agree to make one more attempt. It was our first major challenge as a partnership and was the making of us. Over the course of a hazardous two years we managed to first license and then acquire the lease – thanks to my parents guaranteeing it with their house, a gesture that neither Chris nor I ever forgot.

Nobody expected us to succeed. I even discovered that other restaurateurs had run a sweepstake on how long we would last and no one had put their money on longer than six months. That is one of the reasons I am always suspicious of predictions in any sphere.

It wasn't easy, though. In the early 1980s London had a reputation for poor food in general, and restaurants were stratified along class lines, whereby you had fancy 'toff' restaurants (Michelin, hotels), casual, middle-class ones (brasseries, bistros and trattorias), or more fast-food working-class outlets. In a poll, a sample of the nation's population was asked how often in the average year they went to a proper restaurant – e.g. a 'white tablecloth' one. I still can't believe the answer: less than once a year. (Remember, that includes all the metropolitans going 100+ times per annum.)

With Le Caprice we wanted to create – in both the menu and design – a restaurant that didn't conform to those old class distinctions. Somewhere democratic that served quality food at reasonable prices. But not everyone understood that vision.

I bristled with the reactionary attitudes of the old guard, among them Lord Spencer Churchill, who came through the door and declared at volume, with total insensitivity: 'This place looks like a toilet – it will never work!'

His view was shared by many of the original Caprice clientele. So there I was, back in March 1982, enduring the humbling experience of standing in the restaurant at 9.45 p.m. on a particularly quiet evening with all the 'first sitting' having left and the 'post theatre' not yet arrived. There is always a way through such adversity if you are prepared to work at it, because there is nothing more infectious than personal care and attention, even if there is little accompanying atmosphere. Chris and I were both fortunate to have developed a close clientele in previous restaurants, and the particularly supportive constituency was that of all the theatre practitioners that I had got to know during my time at Joe Allen. They formed a core group that not only provided the liveliness we sought but also the glamour and prestige.

There were very few restaurants in London in the early Eighties that welcomed guests after 10.30 p.m., and even they would often have chairs on the tables by midnight. There was no such time constraint at Le Caprice, and soon the likes of actors Alan Rickman, Hilton McRae, Ian Charleson, Lindsay Duncan, Patricia Hodge, Zoë Wanamaker and casting director Patsy Pollock were making it their home, along with directors, producers and playwrights. But we still needed more. A pivotal moment was when Chris picked up the phone one afternoon to the fashion model Marie Helvin, who said that she was with Mick Jagger and Jerry Hall, Bailey, Bryan Ferry (Jerry's ex!), designer Antony Price and they wanted to come for dinner – would we be busy?

Covering the receiver, Chris relayed to me the question, because we only had about thirty booked for the evening – not busy at all – and what should we do? 'We will be busy,' was my response, and that was relayed to Marie. And so we set about phoning family, friends, non-working staff and told them to get over asap – despite the protests of those who had already eaten or were ready for bed.

When the Helvin party walked in we did indeed appear busy, and just as our own friends were impressed, more importantly so were the bona fide guests who, of course, in turn told their friends what a hot place Le Caprice was, and the story spread.

But still it took time for our concept – modern and fashionable, but casual – to be embraced. Truth is we were getting more support, proportionally, from Manhattan (whether from New Yorkers passing through town or ex-pats) than we were from London. New York had been treated to the newly opened brasserie The Odeon, in Tribeca, which served dry martinis, oysters, steak-frites and omelettes to the likes of Andy Warhol, Tom Wolfe and Jay McInerney, and that led to the support of a generation of artists who immediately understood what we were trying to do with Le Caprice. Then, other creatives started to follow suit and we had the cream of photographers – David Bailey, Terence Donovan, John Swannell, Lords Snowdon and Lichfield (The Queen's cousin), along with writers, publishers, people from the advertising industry and particularly the emerging musicians. This was the time of the post-punk Blitz Club and the goths, and their newfound wealth gave them an appetite for a sympathetic West End experience. Malcolm McLaren, Vivienne Westwood and Steve Strange drew the likes of Boy George and Rusty Egan through to the more mainstream Robert Palmer and Wham!, along with their manager and music producer, Simon Napier-Bell, and influential agents and publicists. Within a year the momentum was evident and it was only a matter of time before the 'old guard' were also arriving – whether the Rolling Stones and surviving Beatles, or Laurence Olivier, Elizabeth Taylor and the ever-important Harold Pinter and Antonia Fraser, who became lynchpins of the place. The adoption of Le Caprice by Diana, Princess of Wales, consolidated our position.

I noted that back when our peers were betting against our success one of the projected reasons was that we would fail 'because of the location', and yet when we confounded prophecy the reason for our success was attributed to . . . the location.

The lesson I've since learned is that if the restaurant is good, it will defy the challenges of location – although a bad location will accelerate the failure of a restaurant that is not 'à point'. This came home to me thirty years or so after we closed and sold our innovative but not success-ful enough restaurant, St Alban. People kindly attributed it to the location (Lower Regent Street), the financial crash of 2008, our modern décor, etc., and although it was tempting to thus attribute, the truth is we just hadn't got it right. St Alban just never really worked – despite being a favourite with many. We tried to be innovative with both the menu and the décor, but it wasn't widely enough understood, notwithstanding that the Mediterranean-inspired food was probably our best ever.

At Le Caprice we were attracting attention and patronage because we dared to be different not only with the design but with the menu and our attitude – and as we owned 100 per cent of the equity no one could tell us otherwise.

One of the reasons why Chris and I have made good partners is that we have come from very different career backgrounds. Chris had the college-taught advantage of knowing how things should work theoret-ically, and I had the contrary advantage of being auto-didact and therefore free of the constrictions of precedent. Chris would suggest the service structure – something I would be so much less adept at – but I would be, in current parlance, the disruptor. And we thrived on it.

Another factor that helped us work together is that we weren't com-petitive. The great secret if you disagree is not to diminish the other's opinion by finding fault, but look for the virtue in the argument. If you can remove the suspicion that the contrary position is motivated by competitiveness, resentment and a desire to be 'right', and can trust each other rather than digging in your heels to assert your position, then you have an opportunity to look for the virtue in the argument and ultimately enhance the decisions you make.

An example of how we disrupted the class-based restaurant system was when I told the floor manager at Le Caprice that I had been to a 'soignée' hotel restaurant the night before; I had been very impressed that once the order was taken there was no one interrupting us to ask 'who's having the chicken?' as they placed the cutlery or when the food arrived. The staff both on the floor and in the kitchen knew who was having what and who the host was, and where the women were sitting (we still aimed to serve women first in those days. Nowadays, one still aims to serve the host last, but the order of service is gender-blind). I asked my manager if he knew how they'd managed it.

'Easy,' he told me. 'There is a system whereby the seats are numbered from the same position on each table. Each number is appended with the order, then a circle is drawn around the numbers which denote female guests, with a square for the host.'

'Brilliant,' I said. 'We're going to do the same . . .'

'Absolutely not,' he said. 'You don't do that in restaurants like this – too complicated, time-taking and inappropriate.'

Oh, but yes, we did. Along with a list of other game-changers. Here is another example. In the Seventies the protocol was that dessert was offered and served with no thought of coffee, or indeed tea, which was offered subsequently. By the time Le Caprice opened, a coffee order might be asked for at the time of dessert but was only ever served when the dessert was cleared. Now this led to problems with Americans, who were used to the notion that, if anything, coffee was served BEFORE dessert, so we would get complaints. The solution seemed to be bringing it sooner, but that led to Brits feeling rushed with the Americans still thinking we were slow. And so this went on. It might seem obvious now, but with my desire to break down precedent and 'the usual', I said, 'Why don't we just ask?' Obvious but elusive, and indeed now this is the norm, and I would delight in this form of change.

Chris and I also achieved a great deal by looking at things that had been done badly for inspiration. This was particularly the case with food, where we took great pride in reinventing modern classics: two of our most popular dishes at Le Caprice were bang bang chicken and Black Forest gateau. Both dishes raised eyebrows when we first introduced them, for they were, at the time, menu clichés: so ubiquitous in restaurants as to have fallen into disrepute. But we made sure our versions tapped into what had made them popular in the first place, and they were soon among our signature dishes.

# 'Those who care, don't count . . .'

In the restaurant business, table allocation is a great source of angst. Early on in my career, I was told by Joe Allen very forthrightly: 'Those who count, don't care – those who care, don't count.'

Joe Allen came into restaurateuring because he was spending too much time drinking away his inheritance at P. J. Clarke's restaurant in New York. He opened Joe Allen in New York's Theater District in 1965, which soon became the successor to the eminent Broadway theatre restaurant Sardi's, and eventually opened outposts around the world, including in London. Despite my immense respect for him, I don't entirely agree with his approach to table allocation. Prestige tables are created as such by the need for privacy and the difficulty of access to them for a passing pesterer or insensitive 'botherer'. The corner table at what was to be my first restaurant, Le Caprice, became famous because we placed the Princess of Wales there. It was somewhat secluded and she could be given a seat where she wouldn't have to catch anyone's eye if she looked up. Privacy and protection were the keynotes. But then it became a competition for

*Joe Allen*

that table, with one of the most avid seekers being the less-than-reticent Jeffrey Archer. And he had 'form' . . .

I am always grateful to one of London's finest maîtres d'hôtel, Angelo Maresca, who presided over the Savoy Grill for twenty-one years in its heyday, up until 2003. His brilliance influenced me in terms of calm rational thinking, and specifically concerning an incident at the Savoy Grill involving the said Lord Archer. It was the 1980s and there was competition for a particular table (let's say Table 7), especially between him and the then high-flying CEO of Guinness, Ernest Saunders, who, at a later date, shared with Archer residency care of Her Majesty's Prison Service. This particular lunchtime, somehow the Grill had taken bookings from both Archer and Saunders, who had both been promised the same table, and the reception staff were quaking.

*Angelo Maresca*

'What shall we do?' the staff asked Maresca. 'First in gets it?'
'No, wait . . .'

And as the clock got closer to 1 p.m. the receptionist was panicking because they were anticipating the tirade of the 'loser' in this battle.

But still Maresca wouldn't give the instructions until he suddenly barked:

'Clear the cutlery and glassware off Table 7 and find the shiniest bucket you can. Put some water in it and place it in the centre of the table, then allocate both Messrs Archer and Saunders elsewhere.'

And to the staff's eternal admiration they watched Maresca greet both parties with the words: 'I am so sorry but there is a ceiling leak above your normal table and we will have to seat you elsewhere accordingly.'

Brilliant.

The best solutions in life are not necessarily elusive, and are often the most simple.

Very often the overwhelming nature of a mini crisis can petrify a manager and render them dumb, when just a little lateral thinking can alleviate the situation. One of my favourite training stories for managers came by courtesy of the legendary Mr Marks of Wiltons in St James's. Not an easy man, and an inveterate snob who famously turned away a single male diner early on a rainy night who had come through the door soaked after a downpour. On asking for a table for himself in an otherwise empty restaurant he was refused by Marks. After the denied customer left, the surprised restaurant manager asked why the refusal when they had space? To which he was told: 'Do we really wish to serve a gentleman who doesn't carry an umbrella?'

But that's not the training story. It is a Friday lunchtime and the then Duke of Devonshire has come through the door, much to Marks's alarm. The Duke's office had an arrangement that Marks would keep the same table every Friday unless he heard from the office that the Duke was not attending that day. So, on entering, the Duke stopped in his tracks on finding that there was a group of four occupying his usual table. Two elegant American couples.

'Marks, who are those people at my table?'

'Your Grace, the reservation was cancelled by your office.'

'Well, I am here, am I not?'

'Yes, your Grace, but I can't move the occupants – all I can offer you is the bar, as every table is taken.'

So the Duke settled and smouldered at the bar, all the time shooting dagger looks at the foursome. He ate quickly, and as he rose to leave he looked first at a large Stilton on the bar and then back at his table, and before the staff could prevent him he had seized the cheese and launched it into the middle of the table, before harrumphing and leaving.

The Americans were left shocked and aghast, covered with wine, food, broken glassware and, of course, cheese. And this is when Marks approached the table.

So I asked my training managers: 'What does he say – what does he do?'

And the answers came in, predictably: 'He apologises.' Of course. 'He offers to pay for the dry cleaning.' Yes, of course. 'He says there will be no charge and invites them back as guests.' Yes, yes, but you are missing the point, which is that there is a question about to be asked by them. Specifically, 'What on earth is going on?'

And there is no viable suggestion from the managers as to how to answer.

What did Marks do?

He said, 'Ladies and gentlemen, my sincere apologies, but please let me explain. The gentleman who threw a Stilton into the middle of your table is His Grace, the Duke of Devonshire. And at Wiltons, the Duke of Devonshire is permitted to throw Stilton.'

There was nothing to be said to that and I am sure the Americans dined out on that story for years. True restaurateuring can never be learned from a textbook.

# Happy problems

None of us has a problem-free life, but it is how we deal with those problems that counts as to whether they have any lasting impact.

When I greet customers, there is a common question:

'Hello, Jeremy. Is everything alright?'

And when my response is 'No!' there is a look of concern. They might ask anxiously what the problem is, and when I reply with, 'Nothing particular', they'll ask why I had said 'no'.

'Because you asked whether *everything* was alright. The answer has to be "No" – the last time I felt everything was alright was probably during the summer of '69 making ice creams in Burnham-on-Sea, when everything felt alright for a couple of weeks. If you had asked me "Is *enough* alright?", I would have said, "Yes – 'Enough' is a good result these days."'

They still think I am going a little mad, but my point is that 'everything' is rarely alright unless perhaps in the first flush of love or success. But that doesn't mean that everything is 'alwrong'. You see, our perceived problems are rarely that serious, as an incident from the early days of Le Caprice brought home to me.

It was sometime in 1982 and I had come in on a Saturday afternoon to get the restaurant open for dinner – we didn't do lunch on a Saturday but the dinner service was an important night for a struggling restaurant. It is indicative of the paucity of business at that time that we used to leave the answerphone on to trap bookings, and there I was writing down the requests from the machine – we could always accommodate people in the early days. But on this occasion the list is too long and I am getting worried because we might not have enough tables and, irritatingly, the phone is still ringing. I eventually get an allocation done, but the time it has taken has set me back and the phone is still interrupting, and meanwhile I am trying to tally the credit card slips and there are more than usual and what with the bloody phone ringing it is difficult to make the summaries. I am starting to get stressed, wishing there weren't so many credit card slips and the phone would stop ringing.

Wait a minute . . .

My problem is that I have more credit card payments than usual and the phone is ringing too much? What sort of a problem is this? And then it dawned on me that these were 'happy' problems and that if I divided my problems in life generally into happy and unhappy, the majority were happy ones. If we are in demand from our friends, for example – we don't have time to see them, are struggling to return their calls, then these are Happy Problems. In this scenario the 'Unhappy Problem' would be to not have the friends, to not receive the calls.

This simple realisation transformed my life, as very little seemed to be catastrophic any more, and when something serious did trouble me, I would have the perspicacity to concentrate my efforts on solving the problem, rather than lamenting it.

# Regrets and instinct

I have many regrets. In fact, I am always suspicious when I read one of those *Sunday Times* interviews when the subject, asked about their own, claims they have none. I don't believe that for a second. I have regrets every day of my life in varying degrees – all I can try to do is avoid dwelling on them. There are moments in particular when I deeply regret a missed opportunity, and normally it is because I was too slow to react, even too cautious, or I didn't trust my instinct sufficiently.

I still shudder for letting down a young diner at Le Caprice in what might seem to be an inconsequential moment but I am sure still haunts him all these years later.

Sitting at a table at the fulcrum of the restaurant was a prominent fashion leader who had decided to bring with them a bright young man from their office, along with another colleague who was entertaining an equally prominent magazine editor. I sensed something wasn't quite right; the young man seemed anxious, daunted by the menu, and he was clearly not enjoying the honour of being at the table. He followed his boss when ordering his first course – a bowl of crudités – only for her to change her mind at the last minute, leaving him with an unknown quantity.

I was caught at another table with a loquacious customer, but the young man's table was in my eyeline and as the story I was being told wound on and on I could see the situation unfold. I watched as the young man studied what he had to eat and saw how perplexed he was by a bowlful of ice studded with vegetables, accompanied by a plate with three ramekins of sauces. I powerlessly listened to the anecdote, as I felt I couldn't interrupt, and I watched him surreptitiously look around the room to see if he could take a lead from someone else eating the same dish – but no such luck. I practically felt the sigh that lifted his chest when, resigned to fate, he took each ramekin and emptied the contents over the bowl of ice and vegetables, then picked up his knife and fork in a disastrous attempt to eat the mess.

As he pressed down on one side of the bowl with his fork, the slick of ice on porcelain flipped the mess of sauces and vegetables over the other side of the bowl. By now I had finally cut short the anecdote, but I was too late to help. The burning cheeks of his humiliation were testimony to my politeness but also my lack of decisiveness.

I still imagine the moment of ignominy haunting that young man, so I am ever alert now to helping people not only in restaurants but in life generally. Wouldn't we all have appreciated being told about the spinach on our teeth, food on our chin, label outside our clothes or skirt tucked into our knickers? However sophisticated we become as a restaurant-going nation there will always be surprises: how do we eat that artichoke, take our fish off the bone, eat asparagus, grapple with a game bird, tackle an oyster, dissect a langoustine, navigate a cheese board (how do I cut into each cheese?)? Or indeed the etiquette of 'sharing-plate' restaurants when the dish only has three items and you are four! Let's try to emulate the grace with which The Queen picked up a finger bowl and affected to drink from it to save the blushes of her guest of honour who had done so.

Being decisive is a skill that eludes the best of us. I posit the following moment of hesitation as a cautionary tale.

This lesson was acquired on the occasion of a live feed from outside Le Caprice of a *Newsnight* discussion about the Princess of Wales. This featured the Bishop of London and the former newspaper editor and presenter, Andrew Neil. It was taking place through an Outside Broadcast Unit at Le Caprice in order to fit in with Andrew Neil's plans. The result of which was that the location was easily discernible on television, which in itself was no harm for Le Caprice, but I came to realise that would possibly not be the case for Andrew Neil . . .

Because in his penthouse flat in Arlington House, above the

restaurant, sat Paul Raymond. A man well known for his Soho sex empire, and indeed, because of its financial success, his ownership of half of Soho. What was less well known was his great love of the monarchy, and we find him getting incensed with what the 'Republican' Andrew Neil is opining as the broadcast goes on. So incensed was Paul that he decided to go downstairs and remonstrate with Neil whilst he was still on air. Paul was ready for bed, but his hurry to get to Neil precluded him dressing. Raymond emerged from the apartment block with his long hair flailing, dressed in a very short and revealing kimono. With a shriek he started running towards Neil. I watched what will surely go down as a great moment of live TV – the sight of Paul Raymond, barely dressed, leaping on Andrew Neil. But, sadly, the producer has a critical second's advantage and was able to intercept the screaming Paul before he reached Andrew. I was too slow to stop the producer stopping Paul. Ever since I have been highly attuned to the potential need to both stop and allow incidents, and to always remain on my toes . . .

Another regret of a different nature comes to mind when I think of the Le Caprice era.

Lauren Bacall – or Betty as she preferred – could be the subject of many a chapter. I first met her in 1985 when she came over to be directed by Harold Pinter in *Sweet Bird of Youth* at the Theatre Royal Haymarket. Pinter would bring her to Le Caprice during rehearsals and post performance. She was immediately charmingly beguiling and fascinating, and I particularly laughed one evening when she raised her elegant forefinger and with it beckoned me to the table. With the same finger she pointed at a new young recruit to our staff and had me bend down so that she could whisper in my ear: 'Oil him. Wrap him. Send him to my room.' I passed on the invitation to the target, but it was politely, and impressively, declined.

My biggest regret, though, with Betty Bacall, came towards the end of the decade, when Chris and I were preparing to open our next restaurant, The Ivy. Betty was filming in London and took a great interest in its theatrical history. She came up with the suggestion that she would do an evening shift as a maître d'hôtel, but without any publicity whatsoever and dressed in uniform like any other member of staff. I loved the idea of guests hearing that voice, seeing those eyes, that stature, and being confused as to how similar this woman was to Lauren Bacall, then it slowly dawning on them all what was happening. My regret? My mistake was that when she offered me two dates I took the later one, instead of grabbing the first opportunity, only to lose her to a sudden death in the family and a premature return to New York.

Always grab those opportunities when offered – immediately – there is never a perfect time.

# The Princess principles

The plain-clothes Special Branch officer flashed his warrant card, introduced himself, then used that tried-and-tested device of delicate disdain – speaking whilst not looking at you. He asked about an innocuous booking the following week, which I confirmed we had, and then asked which table it would be, as the guest was 'somebody very important'. I told him that at this juncture I had no idea where they would be sat; who was this 'very important' guest?

'I can't tell you.'

'Then I can't tell you where they are sitting.'

'But I have to know which table so that we can ensure their safety.'

'Then tell me who's coming, otherwise it looks like they will be eating elsewhere.'

At this he conceded that it was a member of the Royal Family. Knowing the group's host, I decided I would give them the benefit of the doubt and showed him the corner table (then Table 7). On seeing it, the Special Branch officer instructed that we would have to keep the tables on either side vacant and turn the Venetian blinds around the designated one.

'Nope. Seems that whoever they are, they will not be eating here next week.'

With this, he backed down and conceded to my reassurances on safety and privacy.

And a week later, through the door walks Diana, Princess of Wales.

'Why couldn't you just tell me and avoid all the palaver, Ken?'

By now I was on better terms with the legendary Ken Wharfe, head of security for the Princess. His reply was a little sheepish. 'The problem is that after the wedding, when she first went out privately with her friends, she would be taken to restaurants she had previously known and now missed, and we made the mistake of advising the proprietors in advance. Come the day, the owner's wife and her friends would all be at tables in their finest, often with hats, surreptitiously watching every move. Diana would feel uncomfortable every time she looked up. So we started keeping her identity secret until we knew that the restaurateur could be trusted for discretion. I think we'll be fine with you.'

The table that Diana made her own would become the most famous and coveted of any restaurant of its day. It was also the most suitable, for several reasons. In order to get near it, another customer either has to be sitting nearby or beat the protection that is offered by the internal layout. To approach the table is a conscious move and not just a stop on the way to the loo. It also afforded a seat with a sight line through the window, meaning you could have a meal without making eye contact with guests at other tables (unless intended). And of course it needed to be in a good sight line for the security detail, without them being too obviously seen as the protection.

I used to enjoy Diana's arrival because it brought out wonderful British behaviour. As she would come through the door there would be an unmistakable reduction of noise, the general hubbub becoming more of a hum, but otherwise people were very understated; the typical reaction would be, 'Don't look now but Princess Diana has just walked in.' No craning of necks, no staring, with even those sat at the bar, with their backs to the room, able to follow her movement discreetly thanks to the mirrors in front of them. What I would also notice is that once all the eyes had taken in her presence, many pairs would swivel to see how I would respond. Would I come shuffling over like a modern-day Uriah Heep? That's when I would turn to probably the least-known person in the room, followed by others, and only later eventually arrive at the table. And she much preferred it that way – she just wanted to be normal.

As our relationship developed, more opportunities to be normal presented themselves. Before too long, we had started to plan sports events and competitions between Kensington Palace and Le Caprice. My favourite being a Go-Karting challenge we planned. To find us all down near Croydon dressed in the same racing tracksuits was a joy for us both. As we lined up for the competition, the mixture of relative importance or seniority was forgotten by our shared uniform. I respected Diana for her belief in egalitarianism. As it happens, that evening the Palace won the team award, but despite a very spirited and aggressive drive by Diana, the eventual individual winner was a kitchen porter from Le Caprice, who was astonished to find himself being warmly hugged by the Princess upon his victory.

After her separation from Charles, Diana elected to forego private security, and there was many a time that I had to get her away without paparazzi hounding her – back doors, disguises, different car ramps (the car park below Le Caprice had two ramps, one going up and one going down, that could be accessed, without the paps knowing, through the kitchen) – we tried the lot. I would even take the opportunity to water plants or dampen down dust with my garden hose to create a wall of water between us and the paps as she made good her escape.

I also witnessed anguish, tears and despair, and my heart went out to her. It taught me a lesson. The notion that someone with so much could be so unhappy would make many incredulous, but for me it was an early realisation of what I came to understand later; it is not how much you have, but whether you have enough – and I feel Diana would have cherished a simpler 'normal' life.

I watched her carefully on the fateful night in June 1994 as she arrived at the Serpentine Gallery for the *Vanity Fair* Gala Dinner. I had been asked by *Vanity Fair* to cater the dinner, and Diana and I had previously discussed the event. She had told me weeks earlier that she wouldn't be attending, so it was a surprise when I learned the day before that she would be there after all. The penny dropped when I realised the gala was taking place on the same night as ITV were scheduled to broadcast a keenly awaited interview with the then Prince Charles about their marriage. Despite being incredibly shy, Diana was a canny player of the press when needed.

Another surprise had blindsided me an hour or so before her arrival, when I was standing by the marquee, deep in thought. I had come over to offer moral support and check that our operations director Robert

Holland and chef Mark Hix were okay. I was deep in thought because earlier in the day Chris Corbin had undergone a bone marrow transplant to try to save him from leukaemia. My mind had gone back to the week before when I had celebrated my fortieth birthday, also under the auspices of Robert and Mark, and I had broken down whilst making my speech because of Chris's absence and the uncertainty of what lay ahead for him.

My reverie was interrupted by a cheery 'Hello, Jeremy', and I looked up to see Princess Diana's bodyguards, all in black tie (Ken Wharfe had resigned six months previously).

'You are looking very smart,' I said. 'Where have you been?'

'Nowhere,' came the reply. 'This is a black tie event – surprised you aren't changed yet.'

Of course it was! I should have known.

'Oh well, I'm not involved in the service, so no need.'

'Yes, there is. You should know the protocol by now. This marquee is technically your "building" and therefore, as ever, you have to greet any major Royal and escort them to their table.'

I did know this, but hadn't thought it would apply to a tent in the park. This was a problem, and the only solution was to go home to Islington to change, then get back within an hour in order to fulfil my duties. Luckily, I had an early mobile phone and a scooter, so having phoned ahead to ask for help getting my garb out, I was able to speed home, get changed, and make it back to the Serpentine Gallery just ten minutes before the Princess arrived in what would become known as her 'revenge dress' – a sleek, black, off-the-shoulder dress with a sweetheart neckline.

However much she sparkled that night, her aura seemed to me dulled, and she whispered her apprehension to me as I led her through. And although she seemed to achieve freedom with the divorce, she never was able to properly soar like a bird released from its cage in the years after.

At her funeral in Westminster Abbey on 6 September 1997, I watched, almost numb, as the insecurities of too many around me took flight. The seating was an issue: it was arranged in blocks with the allocation within them being quite random – there hadn't been time for the Palace to attempt a detailed placement – and the jealousy sparked over who sat in the front row while others were 'relegated' to further back was toxic. Whilst there was much genuine distress and sadness among the congregation, some factions seemed to have forgotten why they were there. An element of the fashion crowd was treating the aisle as if it were a catwalk, while other guests wouldn't take their seats, despite entreaties from ushers, preferring to socialise rather than pay their respects. Also noticeable was how certain members of the Royal Family fumed while obliged to stand uncomfortably in front of us in the aisle as their grand exit ground to a halt while waiting for Charles to leave. He himself was stunned into immobility, taken aback by the crowd's reaction.

All of our human frailties and uncontained self-interest were on display when we should have been commemorating and celebrating someone who eschewed the privileges and grandeur of royalty and would have been happier living a more humble life.

# Part 2: 1990s, The Ivy

# Lessons from The Ivy

In 1977 I stood outside what was then a dusty, archaic, failing husk of a restaurant on West Street, in Covent Garden, called The Ivy and declared to my friend John Maxwell that, 'If ever I own a restaurant, it will be this one.' John had introduced me to The Ivy some months earlier and I'd since been back several times; there was something special about this old grand dame, even in her current ailing condition. My assertion would prove prescient, although it would be more than a decade before it came to pass.

Chris and I were buoyed by the success of Le Caprice and began actively seeking a sibling restaurant in 1983. We approached the owners of The Ivy and were turned down, so we expanded our search. We were looking for something special, and for several years we were thwarted. We had tried The Criterion in Piccadilly Circus (recently rescued from its formica cladding as part of the 'Golden Egg' restaurant chain) and had failed to secure A L'Ecu de France on Jermyn Street, which had originally been under the same ownership of Caprice and the now-disappeared Empress.

We tried again with The Ivy, which was in the hands of Lew Grade's family, but although the restaurant was going under, they didn't seem to want to sell to us. Eventually, after failed annual approaches, I was called by our agent, David Coffer, and asked whether I knew The Ivy and that it was for sale. (Fascinating that the Grade family didn't come to us directly – maybe the old British begrudging of someone succeeding where you have not?) So I asked how much for and I think £700,000 was the quote – a bargain, as the lease had a further twelve years to run at almost peppercorn-like rent. 'We'll take it,' came my immediate response. 'You don't want to see it?' he asked. 'I have been looking at it for over ten years,' I replied, and an offer at the asking price was made. From thereon I learned the first of my Ivy lessons, because we then got into an auction with a mysterious bidder. The price was going up rapidly in £100,000 bids and was already at £1.3 million. Before putting in another, even higher, bid, I realised I should ask a question:

'Who is the other bidder?'

'We don't know.'

'Shouldn't you find out?'

'We can't – the agent is in a confidentiality agreement.'

'C'mon, David – you are better than to allow that to thwart you!'

Subsequently he came back rather embarrassed . . .

'It's the landlord.'

'And who is that?'

'Mark Knopfler of Dire Straits.'

'What? Who knew he was into property?'

Turned out that he very much was, and with his advisor (accountant Ronnie Harris) he had bought The Ivy building and wanted to buy in the lease in order to grant a new lease which could be coterminus with the other leases in the building – twenty-five years – and charge a proper commercial rent.

'Then let him have it! Let's switch to a Dutch auction and hopefully he will get it at £700k and then let it to us.' And that worked . . .

Next bit of learning was negotiating the lease with our fearless lawyer, Michael Gien, fronting up. It is so important to have someone without emotion calling the shots – because otherwise you will make the mistake that I nearly made. The equally fearsome lawyers for Mark and Ronnie were demanding a personal guarantee from Chris and myself and said it was a deal breaker. Frankly, I would have given them anything, and it was excruciating when Michael dug his heels in and refused. 'Please, Michael, let them have it – it's fine,' I pleaded, and he bluntly responded that as long as he was my lawyer he would never allow me to sign a personal guarantee. And of course, not for the first time, he was right.

We duly completed on the lease and set about the refurbishment, and it wasn't long before we ran out of money and had to persuade Hambros Bank to keep funding us. Each time I ran out of ways to finagle more money from them I would find another baffling explanation, and time after time I somehow managed to avoid the need to sell equity to complete the project.

Some months after we opened, once trading was getting good, Hambros called a meeting and hesitatingly explained that they were looking for some substantial extra fees – circa £40,000 then, which equates to about £100,000 now. Their logic was that they really shouldn't have lent us so much money on the security we had and they should have been entitled to equity.

They were absolutely right, but my inherent belief in a way to find a solution to any problem found me saying: 'Please don't ask me this. I really like working with you and I would hate to have you drop me as a customer.'

'But we're not planning to?'

'But you'll have to.'

'Why?'

'Because if one of your clients was to freely accede to a request for such a large amount of money when they had no need to, it would denote that they are financially irresponsible and shouldn't be running a company nor be your client. That would be such a shame.'

And, seemingly bamboozled, they dropped the claim.

The artists we wanted to do site-specific art for the interior were commissioned, and thanks to art dealer Leslie Waddington's gallery and other friends we had an impressive roster of leading 'Pop Art' and contemporary artists. Peter Blake did one of his 'assemblages' of painting, photography and objects, etc. Michael Craig-Martin contributed a painting and the 'knife & fork' framed, stained-glass clock in the turret. Tom Phillips did a wonderful wall of paintings of Modernists who had been in different careers before finding their métier (Rousseau the douanier, Chekhov the doctor), as well as an etched-glass dividing wall and the menu cover. Allen Jones provided a mural across the rear of the restaurant, Eduardo Paolozzi the metal staircase handrail frieze, Patrick Caulfield the prominent stained-glass window on the 'prow', with other works from Bill Jacklin and Bridget Riley, and even a painting by David Bailey.

Howard Hodgkin had promised a large, defining painting above the prime table in the room on the best sightline. What he delivered was an oval green print that he had worked an ivy leaf into. It was fine enough, but because it was printed on paper it had to be protected under Perspex, which in turn rendered the piece difficult to see because of the reflection. When we questioned it not being the commission we had instructed, Howard went off on us, saying that he was trying to evoke the shiny glaze of a plate and that we were philistines for not understanding, and it was typical of the paucity of cultural sophistication in Europe. How we argued over that one!

But even with the challenges that they sometimes created, we were enormously proud of all the original artwork in the restaurant, which today, sadly, have been mostly separated and scattered.

Not everyone was keen to participate, though. Marc Quinn's agent played hardball on price and I still smile when I think of John Hoyland's retort: 'Who wants hairdressers leaning their greasy hair against their paintings?'

There were plenty of other challenges to come. I recall a conversation with the Hambros bank manager, who was getting nervous about their exposure.

'Is there any press interest?'

'Yes, in fact I don't think there is a magazine nor broadsheet that hasn't shown interest.'

'When will we be seeing the articles?'

'You won't – we have declined.'

'Are you sure that's wise? And will there be an opening party – celebrities coming?'

'There will be a party, but only for suppliers, contributors, builders, architects.'

I tried to assuage his anxiety by explaining that the prevalent feeling in the UK at that time (1990) was that if you hype something there was a sense of 'tall poppy syndrome'. And if we were to have a party we would invite 200 and upset 2,000. Things have changed now with social media, but I still believe that the best publicity for enduring success is word of mouth and discretion.

The Ivy is considered to have been packed to the gills from the off, but in truth the opening night we served forty-six covers (at its peak, over 300 was a good night). That same night, the IRA bombed the Junior Carlton Club, a gentlemen's club on Pall Mall, sending shock-waves through the city, with people scared to venture out of their homes, and throwing the hospitality industry into a frenzy. Opening for Saturday lunch subsequently, we actually did a 'zero'. What I mean is that we went through a service without a single guest. Tragic, and very hard. Not many people have experienced that. In the theatre you can just shut up shop and go home if no one attends, but in a restaurant you have to stand for the duration with an anticipatory smile before you let it drop. However, the way you respond is crucial. You clearly and critically examine what you are doing but you resist the temptation to listen to all the people who will feel they know better – keep the clarity, maintain the belief. And you stand shoulder to shoulder with the staff at all times.

Even when the going was tough in those early days, we resisted the temptation to publicise widely. I was asked by the maître d'hôtel of The Ivy why the recently reopened, highly publicised Quaglino's in St James's was receiving so much more attention than The Ivy, even in his hometown of Manchester. I explained that I felt that the people in Manchester or London who we wanted to know would do, and we must hold our nerve. It is what I call 'narrow-casting' rather than 'broadcasting', and whilst it takes longer to produce the numbers, the type of guest is more suited to our ambitions. At The Ivy it started to work, and then it suddenly took off; it was the rediscovery of the legendary place by the theatre profession that did it.

The biggest lesson was then to protect what we had created, and in the spirit of how the greatest restaurant critic of the time, AA Gill, explained it, not to allow any single 'tribe' to dominate a room. It was fun for Harold Pinter to have David Beckham or similar sat next to him from time to time, but if there were several footballer tables then the atmosphere would change and Pinter would not enjoy being there – especially if they had commandeered his favourite table. It was great to have the leaders of the advertising industry, for instance, but not good if it became a media canteen and there were too many ad people.

It also became clear to me that we had to control advance bookings. Standing in the reservations room in January 2000, I heard a typical conversation taking place.

'No, I am afraid we are full this Saturday. On Friday too – and next Saturday too, and for the rest of the month.'

And I knew what was coming next as a question from the potential customer – 'When is the first available table for four at 8.30 p.m. on a

Friday or Saturday night?' But I had to leave before I heard the answer. Checking with the receptionist later as to what the answer was, he said, 'May'. I was a little surprised, only four months, until he clarified that it was May 2001 – sixteen months away . . .

'Then we must stop this system because people are coming for the wrong reason – for a show rather than the conviviality of eating in a restaurant, and the atmosphere will plummet.' It is important that we remember the necessity of curation for everyone's sake. From then on I stopped the notion of 'next available' tables and stipulated that only three dates could be asked for.

Somehow, we managed ten years of fun, conviviality and celebrity, but there were moments I will always remember and certainly learned from.

**Discretion:** If ever you see me in one of my restaurants twice in a day, or two days running, don't be surprised if I greet you as if it is for the first time – that is, until you mention it – because you might have just told your host/guest that you have been so busy you haven't been out . . . As happened the last time I made this mistake in the early Nineties. A regular guest had been in at lunch on a Friday and I had talked with them for a while, including discussing their weekend plans, only to find them unexpectedly back in the evening, which had caught me by surprise. It led me to say, 'I hadn't expected to see you so soon!', at which three heads at the table turned sharply towards her.

As she explained later, the problem had arisen because after lunch she was due to have an afternoon meeting with three clients who were keen to make a fuss of her and take her out for dinner. 'We are so excited as we have managed to secure a booking at The Ivy tonight. You haven't been there recently, have you?' And she had foolishly panicked and said no rather than disappoint them. As she said herself: lesson learned. Always think of the ramifications of what you might say at any time.

**Questions, not statements:** One of the most important pieces of advice I find myself giving is the importance of asking questions, because it is the route to the solution of problems rather than an escalation of them. Witness this scenario one evening when the central large table in the restaurant included Julian Belfrage – gregarious theatrical agent to the likes of Daniel Day-Lewis and Judi Dench, and previously Michael Whitehall's business partner. Julian enjoyed a life that was tragically cut short, and on this particular evening he was at the end of a big meal and holding court while smoking a cigar. From a nearby table approached an American who walked right up to Julian, poked him in the shoulder and said: 'I am about to eat my food, so you are going to put that cigar out NOW!' prodding Julian yet again. Julian coolly watched the man return to his table with a noticeable swagger, jutting his jaw out, and sit down, saying, 'That told him.' Then Julian slowly stood up and approached the man just as he was starting to eat his pasta, and very deliberately and forcefully ground out the remains of his cigar into it. This sparked a fight, which we quelled, but the manager was adamant that we accede to the American's demands that Julian should be expelled. 'On the contrary,' I told him. 'It was the American who was the aggressor – he has to go. There were other options open to him without a confrontation, such as asking.'

And that's the nub of it, if you ask you might get. He could have asked Julian would he mind stopping smoking whilst he ate, or indeed asked the restaurant to move him. Questions get the point across less confrontationally than accusations or dogma.

**Humour:** I have been told that I appear to be rather a serious man, even though inside I might be feeling the opposite. At The Ivy I once happened to be watching as a waiter, holding a tray of food, was quickly walking up to the station just beyond a table of six who were to be the recipients. They received the food in an unconventional way, though, because just as the waiter was about to pass the table one of the guests pushed back their chair into his path, which stopped him dead, but not the tray's momentum as it tipped forward. And in what seemed like slow motion I watched four lobster bisques catapult into the air and land on the table, with the underplates and other food following. You can imagine the mayhem, but the horrified waiter and nearby staff couldn't have anticipated my reaction. I started to giggle . . . what else was there to do? Even the guests found that infectious because they quickly realised it was their own fault and there was no one to blame. Of course, we made good all that we could and found the mutual humour in the situation rather than all get over-excited. I feel therein is the solution to many dramas – to see the comedy.

**Do not be impressed by money:** This particular evening in 1994 we had a group in from the premiere of a film called *True Lies*, which was starring Arnold Schwarzenegger and Jamie Lee Curtis, who were at the table. As was the norm, the 'stars' would be introduced on stage before the film at the cinema in Leicester Square, then make a run for dinner at The Ivy, finish up in time to return to the cinema for the applause at the end of the screening, and then go on to an after-party. There were others in the group, but what was preoccupying me was a swarthy man standing near the table.

'What are you doing?' I asked him, and he said he was with the star table. 'You can't stand there,' I said, and he indicated that he was carrying a gun. 'Now you definitely have to go – that's not even legal.' To which he shook his head, saying that if he went so would the whole group. 'Then it's goodbye to all of you.'

At this point Robert Earl, founder and CEO of restaurant group Planet Hollywood, interceded, asking what the problem was.

'No problem as such because this guy is telling me you are all leaving anyway because I have told him to get out – and I am not impressed that he claims he is packing a gun.'

Robert realised that I was angry and told the bodyguard to 'get the fuck out', then came back to smooth over the situation. He reminded me of the roster of guests: 'You know Arnie and Jamie Lee, I am sure, and Sylvester [Stallone] of course and that's James Cameron – the best film director in the world.'

'Best director in the world? By what criteria do you adjudge that?'

'*The Terminator* films are the biggest-grossing – what other criteria can there be?'

'Well, that's where we have different beliefs and criteria.'

It sounds naïve now, but I was rattled. Up until this point I had thought that achievement could not be defined by money. All of a sudden I understood an actor friend who had told me about a Hollywood dinner party they'd attended where there had been a pecking order determined by box office. I began to realise that this credo was becoming more prevalent in the UK, and that displays of wealth, 'Rich Lists' and assets were becoming more the arbiter of success than critical achievement. To this day I lament this situation and try to be sure that money is never the definer of worth or talent – look for the artistry, creativity, aura and beauty of people and 'things' and you will have a greater appreciation of life.

# Decisions

As the end of her time at university approached, Hannah, my elder daughter, came to me to talk careers. This was after the completion of a holiday stint at The Wolseley (we'll come to that).

'Dad, I really need to decide what to do with my life. The truth is that I hadn't expected to enjoy working in the restaurants so much, and I'm told I am doing well (*she was – extremely*). So I am thinking maybe I should join you in the business – what do you think?'

'Absolutely not – no chance,' I said.

She looked crestfallen. 'That's a bit harsh. Why not?'

'Because you used the word "should". And without question just about everything I regret in my life has been something I did because I felt I "should". I am only interested in "wants" and I fear for you kids being terrorised by the pressure of expectation. You *want* to be a theatre director and that's what you must do if you are in the pursuit of happiness. However, if that doesn't work out and you come back to me in three years and tell me you really *want* to join me, then I will welcome you with open arms and pride.'

She didn't come back.

How I wish I had listened to my own advice. Sometimes I am good at these dilemmas and, by way of example, I look back to the moment that I realised the crucial part it plays in our lives.

It was the early Nineties and we were building The Ivy's reputation and success when I got a call from Mark Knopfler, The Ivy's landlord.

He asked, 'Do you know the Bluebird ambulance garage on the King's Road?'

'Of course.'

He went on: 'Do you think it would make a good restaurant?'

'We've all been driving past it for years fantasising about what an amazing restaurant it would make.'

'Do you want it?'

'Duh – of course . . .'

'Then meet me tomorrow at 11 a.m. – it's yours, I bought it this morning.'

With a heady excitement Chris and I duly met Mark and did a tour. Oh my, it was beautiful, especially the first-floor room.

'So do you want it?' Mark asked.

'Well, yes, but we need to discuss the rent . . .'

'The rent will be below market so no need to worry about that. I want you to do this.'

'That's kind, but Mark, we hadn't realised the scale of the building and we just won't be able to afford the cost of development without selling equity – and we don't want to do that.'

'Don't worry about the finance – I will fix that. Will you take it?' He was determined.

'Well, the other aspect is that this ground floor goes back so far, and well beyond the scope of a restaurant. It needs retail, and that's not our expertise.'

He wasn't going to be thwarted: 'Don't worry about that – we will underwrite the retail but you can have control on who it is let to. Will you take it?' he asked, somewhat exasperated.

I said that Chris and I needed to confer. We moved away to the end of the beautiful room and looked each other in the eye, knowing that this was going to be our next project.

Or was it?

I asked Chris, 'What do you think?' – almost rhetorically, I felt.

'We should do it – what about you?'

'You're right – we should do it.'

And, fortunately, as I turned to go and give the news to Mark, I hesitated, and looking back at Chris asked, 'Do you *want* to do it?'

'No,' he replied, without missing a beat. 'Do you?'

'No.' Our eyes locked. 'Then what the hell are we doing?'

As we explained our answer to an incredulous Mark, a credo was formed for the future about how we would make decisions. And the driving themes that have helped me in my decision-making process: 'No one will criticise me if I don't do this project – but if I do it and I get it wrong then I have to reckon on the damage of public opinion.'

It was imperative to always ask ourselves: are we acting because we feel we *should,* or because we truly *want* to do so? I believe that the more we feel we have the responsibility for the happiness of others – to the detriment of our own – the greater the problems we create. Just as the airline announcement reminds you to put on your own oxygen mask before going to the aid of others, the same must apply to our supply of happiness.

I tell my children to bear in mind the 'Dinner Party Test' when considering career moves. I ask them to imagine being at a dinner with, say, ten guests and finding themselves sat next to a stranger who at some point will ask them what it is they do for a living. Just at that moment imagine the table falls quiet and everyone will hear your reply. When you say what you do, do you feel pride in your answer, and do you give it without qualification, justification or explanation? If you can imagine that being the case, then you might well have found the right role.

On the question of pleasing yourself versus pleasing others, I think too of Ed Victor, one of the greatest literary agents of our time, who sadly died in 2017, and I miss him terribly. Ed was an uncompromising American, born in the Bronx, who was instrumental in changing the way British publishing thought of literary agents, and he achieved some of the most spectacular deals whilst also being the first to increase his commission from 10 per cent to 15 per cent. He had a vast array of qualities, talents and skills, and although modesty wasn't one of them – I particularly smile remembering him saying to me one day, 'That's enough about you – let's talk about me.' He was, however, a font of good sense and pragmatic advice. One story that has underwritten my life since he recounted it concerned the making of decisions. I always worried about offending, disappointing or annoying someone through rejection, but Ed managed to emancipate me through this tale.

He was at a party and was approached by the infamous but rather fun socialite Claus von Bülow.

'Ed, just the man I was hoping to see. I wanted to talk to you about my friend (let's call him Count von Indolent). He has written a fascinating memoir and I think that you would be just the person to represent him in getting it published.'

This was not an unusual occurrence for Ed – the literary agent's equivalent of a doctor being asked for a cocktail party diagnosis. But he said, by all means Claus's friend should send the manuscript over.

And of course it was turgid and of no interest, but Ed dutifully wrote to 'Count von Indolent' and explained that it wasn't right for him. He suggested another (less-discerning) agent and also proposed (rather savagely) that maybe self-publishing would be the best route.

But the problem was that with their social circle it was inevitable that Ed would not be able to avoid running into Claus, and when that eventually happened Ed immediately confronted the issue.

'Claus, I am so sorry that I couldn't help Count von Indolent more with his memoir but . . .' and Claus cut him off. 'No explanation needed.' Ed tried to go on, 'I know that you placed great store in me . . .' And again Claus cut him short, saying: 'I will not have you apologising. You behaved impeccably and gave the second-best answer.'

'Second-best answer?'

Claus went on: 'Of course the best answer is a "yes", but if that's not possible then the second-best is a "quick no".'

And there the key to being liberated from the agony of procrastination was gifted to me. Unless you are genuinely unsure, always make your 'nos' quick ones, because the seemingly kind 'That's an interesting idea – let me think about it' only leads to false hope and agonising delays in telling the truth.

The question of 'I should' or 'I want' extends to social engagements, too. In a world where we have so many invitations to decide between, alongside obligations and duties, it can be a dilemma knowing what to accept and what to decline.

How often have you agreed to do something in the future and then as the day approaches regretted it? Why did you accept? Was it through obligation, guilt or even fear of missing out? I have three simple rules that seem to resonate with those I share them with:

1) Never accept to do in the future anything that you wouldn't be happy to be doing this evening.
2) When declining, always give a quick no.
3) Never give an excuse or explanation.

On that third point, the saying goes: 'Your friends don't need it, and your enemies won't believe it . . .'

# Honesty

After opening The Ivy in 1990 I was particularly busy trying to cope with the demands of the new restaurant while still getting round to Le Caprice to see the customers. And I was fast realising that I was turning into the type of obsequious, sycophantic restaurateur that I abhorred. In a desire to make people happy, I was saying anything to please them – which often meant I was lying. It had to stop, otherwise I would lose my reputation for authenticity and simply become a cipher.

So I made a vow: I would never tell a lie. Not even a white one.

My vow was immediately put to the test, as almost within minutes I was walking into The Ivy and found myself talking to a lady I knew quite well at the time, who was sporting a new hairstyle. After a while she declared: 'Jeremy, you haven't mentioned my hair – and I know you notice everything.'

There was good reason for my silence on the subject – her hair was truly a disaster. I reckoned she knew it and was looking for the reassurance that my honesty pledge wouldn't allow.

'I am afraid I must admit that I preferred it the way you had it before.'

Neat, I thought, not as offensive as 'I don't like it' – but this did not go down well with the exposed, insecure questioner: 'Well, I will know not to ask YOU in future – all my friends love it.'

'Then you must rely on them,' I said as I slipped away – but not into any respite. Next up was a table of investors and producers hosted by theatre owner and producer Michael Codron. It was the day after the opening of Michael Palin's play *The Party* in Codron's theatre, The Aldwych. Mischievously, he called me over. 'This is Jeremy, everyone – Jeremy, didn't I see you at the opening last night? What did you think?'

I say 'mischievously' because he knew full well that I had slipped away at the interval, and here I am facing five investors who are hanging on to the hope that the faintly positive review in *The Express* might gain more credence than the lukewarm ones elsewhere. They know the play is a complete dog but they are going to indulge themselves by hearing me utter meaningless platitudes to reassure themselves and pretend it will be ok. Or so they think. But I can't indulge them as I am not allowed to under my new regime.

'Well, I cannot tell a porky pie,' I said. 'I didn't like it at all.' Crestfallen looks as I am not playing the game. 'However, I am pretty sure your money is safe and it will run . . .' They perked up at this and Michael said that I had done exactly the right thing, because they all dropped the pretence that it was good, then they relaxed and toasted the public who would still make it at least a comparative commercial success. And it was.

I was beginning to enjoy this new persona, and two days later I found a fresh version of the challenge at Le Caprice as I approached another regular, Mo Rothman, who had had the prescience to buy the entire Charlie Chaplin catalogue and thrived accordingly. He asked me if I knew his guest and indeed I did. He was a bigoted, arrogant man who I couldn't stand, and here was Mo saying that he had been complaining that he couldn't get a reservation, and when he did, it wasn't a 'good table'. Now this is tricky because I know the question that is coming next: 'Why is that?'

I have three options:

1) 'I am sorry – we have been terribly busy' (means nothing)
2) 'I am sorry – please leave me a message if ever that happens' (might work)
3) 'I am sorry – here's my card – never let that happen again' (sincere)

But I can't even go to the basic response – because I am *not* sorry – and this is where British humour came to my rescue.

'It's simple – we don't like you and we don't want you in the restaurant,' I said, but with a smile, which denotes that I am joking. After
all, surely I wouldn't say that seriously, it must be the old British way of
being the rudest to those that you love the most? And when they
laughed, I doubled down and said, 'No, I meant it – can't stand you!',
eliciting even more laughter and an assumption that I would remedy
the situation.

Which I didn't.

And so I was emancipated by 'truth', and I quickly learned that not
ever lying doesn't mean that you have to offer up the actual truth –
unless tinged with a big dollop of irony.

# Integrity

Maintaining success in our industry relies on integrity. But challenges to one's integrity come in many forms, especially if you are successful. I have seen customers cheated in so many ways because the opportunity is just too tempting for too many restaurateurs or managers. I have seen cheap cognac poured over ice cream when the request was for vintage Armagnac. Yes, it is a foolish ask, but the rationalisation that 'they will never know' doesn't justify the cheat at all. Nor when an affluent guest has phantom bottles added to their bill. Nor when food that is recovered from a dropped plate is 'dusted off'. Just because they won't know doesn't make the cheat acceptable.

The notion of this imperative for honesty became clear to me when renovating The Ivy in 1989. We were so over budget because every time we opened up panelling or walls, there would be a new surprise. A good example would be the famous diamond designed windows – all stained glass and lead. In my budget I had allowed for £2,500 to repair them (it was 1989!) and had already spent £27,000 and only fixed 40 per cent of them. How could we rein in the spending? Our architect – the late MJ Long – said that one solution was to save on the expensive American oak panelling for any sections of the wall where we were hanging large art commissions. 'No one will know,' she said.

'But *we* will know, and that makes me very uncomfortable.'

And it is true that in the event of the Joe Tilson in the bar or the Howard Hodgkin in the dining room being damaged, then *everyone* would know. The friend of integrity is authenticity, and without these we soon get found out in life. So never cheat, and not because you fear being found out but because you are ultimately the one who has to hold their head up high.

This comes into play in different ways. I am often asked about whether I would serve particular despots, tyrants, fascists or felons, and integrity has a central role in that decision. Fortunately, we rarely have to make an on-the-spot decision because any visit by, let's say, a Trump or similar is heralded and we can decline gracefully, or not. However, I recall a dilemma that Ruthie Rogers was faced with at The River Cafe. The restaurant had taken a large table booking for a late lunch and when the group arrived there was one clearly central figure, with the rest of the party comprising of obsequious men. Ruthie could tell it was someone notionally important, but couldn't work out who they were, until a customer said: 'You know that is Augusto Pinochet.' Pinochet, the despicable tyrant of Chile, who was anathema to Ruthie in every way. On the phone she was saying that she couldn't take his money, but at the same time, of course, she couldn't 'comp' him. In asking what she should do we came up with a solution – take the money and give it to his victims' charities.

No matter who we are dealing with we must act with integrity. If there is someone behaving badly, bullying the servers, harassing the female staff, it doesn't matter how famous, rich, influential or scary they are, they need to be treated the same as anyone else. We might lose business and make enemies, but in protecting our colleagues we preserve our integrity – which will help us endure and succeed.

# Confidence

I often speak of the need for authority in what we do. If we show confidence, then we get results. Ultimately, we want to believe in others and have that belief shown in ourselves.

I discovered this over the years in the restaurant business by realising that the clearer the vision, the easier success could be achieved. It became immensely obvious when conceiving the menu for J. Sheekey, the third restaurant Chris and I acquired, back in 1998. J. Sheekey was a fish restaurant in Covent Garden (not five minutes from The Ivy) that had been established in 1896 and had fallen into disrepair and disrepute. Although it had a set of rooms that were really problematic for service logistics, we felt that we must be able to rekindle the flame that had once made it great.

It was also an important lesson in following your instinct – in this case, mine. I had issued a brief to our property agent, David Coffer (who sadly passed in 2024), for a new restaurant which stipulated 7,500 square feet on one floor, with one large room. He had found a couple that filled the spec, but I had rejected them. And now I was calling him to say that the search was off as we had found the perfect site and would he act on our behalf? He was surprised to hear we had found something he was unaware of, and even more so when I told him it was J. Sheekey.

'What the fuck?!' he yelled at me, not for the first or last time. 'Your brief is 7,500 square feet, one room, one floor. What are you talking about? Sheekey's is 3,500 square feet, five rooms, two floors. Are you mad?'

'Yes, but I like it . . .'

So there I was explaining to the team that we were going to make it a fish-only restaurant. Nearly everyone disagreed with me, and in turn many a customer worried, too. 'You have to have some meat dishes', 'Nobody will come to a fish-only restaurant', 'It will never work'. But I was resolute that it would be in the tradition of fish restaurants like Overton's, Wheelers, Café Royale in Edinburgh, or indeed my favourite, English's of Brighton. The only person apparently not nonplussed was the man who had to produce it – head chef Tim Hughes.

'Tell me more,' he said. 'What sort of fish?'

'Well, I want it more British than anything. I don't want "Grilled Mahi-Mahi with a mango salsa" or suchlike.'

He warmed to the challenge.

'So are you saying effectively that we only use fish and seafood found in British coastal waters – maybe going down into the Channel?'

'Exactly that, if possible,' I told him, as I was also getting excited when Tim said he could make that work.

And it was the best menu I think we ever created. The constriction crystallised and concentrated our thinking and brought creativity, innovation and classicism to what was an old-fashioned concept. All the doomsayers were confounded and we had a great success, as the restaurant was loved by the traditionalists as well as the avant-garde and the theatre world. (Sadly, that clarity is no longer in the restaurant's current incarnation, but Tim is deservedly the estimable Executive Chef of Caprice Holdings Group and is owed a great debt of gratitude by us all.)

Here I must pause for a small digression on how a restaurant's identity can be shaped by factors outside your control. Not long after opening Sheekey's, I was talking to Serena Sutcliffe and David Peppercorn, *the* power couple of the wine trade – and Serena was asking me how the recent opening of the restaurant compared with those of Le Caprice and The Ivy, the sister restaurants of Sheekey's.

'Well, it's funny you ask,' I said, 'because it is very different. Both Caprice and Ivy would be full of customers regaling me about how their parents, grandparents, family or friends had met, got engaged, celebrated birthdays and anniversaries in the original iterations of the restaurants – the role they had in family life. Whereas at J. Sheekey there was virtually no mention nor discussion of family other than the occasional man telling me how his father had sometimes brought him into the restaurant.'

'Well, you know why that is, don't you?' laughed Serena. 'It's because it was always a seduction restaurant, and never the twain would meet. Just like Lapérouse in Paris. Have you ever been? No? It was *the* restaurant for clandestine affairs and even had several small private rooms like railway carriage compartments which had a table, two chairs, a chaise-longue, a bell and a lock on the door.'

Now I was fascinated.

She went on: 'But the best bit was the main dining room. It was a square room with large mirrors and the tables were set out around the edge with occupants sat side by side – only fours in the middle. Now, said mirrors were badly scratched and strangely tatty for such a grand restaurant, but there was a good reason for this, all to do with the place's raison d'être. It was prestigious for a man to have a mistress, to be seen to be virile, and the prettier the lover or concubine the greater the prestige of the liaison.

'But this comes at a cost. And there is an expectation of gifts, so whenever a beautiful diamond ring was slid across the table the recipient would open the box and whilst slipping the diamond ring on her finger make all the right noises of appreciation: "*Oh cherie, c'est charmant, si belle,*" etc., but at the same time reaching behind and running the "rock" down the mirror to ascertain whether it was real, and hence cutting into the glass. And then the greatest aphrodisiac seemed to be when the lover cut the initials of the benefactor into the mirror for all to see!'

Sadly, in the recent refurbishment they got rid of the mirrors.

But now I was learning, and of course I was observing the more modern-day etiquette of illicit love or, more accurately, liaisons. I realised there were many more restaurants being 'catalysts for love'. Take the example of Kettner's, in Soho, which also had hotel rooms. In the Fifties and Sixties, if a lunch was presenting an opportunity of something post-prandial, then asking the head waiter for 'a special' would ensure a room key tucked into the bill folder and a suitably disguised charge as an extra bottle of wine on the bill. Manzi's, when at the original Leicester Square site, offered the same facility and, of course, it is well recorded that there is always the expedience of a broom cupboard at Nobu if you can't 'get a room'.

But why did such liaisons all play out in public, and often at popular and busy restaurants where the chance of discovery increased? It goes back to the aphrodisiacal properties of the male buck being seen to 'win' in the more genteel rutting stakes. And the truth is that many will use the notion that if they were to be caught in a lower-division Italian that 'no one' goes to then the subterfuge would be obvious, whereas taking your lover to somewhere like The Ivy plays the 'hidden in plain sight' card – 'If I was having an affair would I be conducting it at The Ivy? Don't be silly!'

As a restaurateur I don't like this. It makes me sad, and also often angry, especially if it's a friend who, with a look, feels they can make me complicit and expects me to play along when I next see their partner. So if you feel you must, please think about everyone it affects and ask whether it is worth it.

Back to the question of confidence. Indecision induces fear or dissent, and a fascinating aspect of humanity is how much we want to be led. This is dangerous, of course, but if we examine the great state leaders they have been imbued with massive confidence. The only problem is that it also becomes the province of the dictator or despot.

This comes in many forms, but at its simplest I illustrate by the example of there, let's say, being a group lost in the jungle with diminishing resources and dwindling strength and resolve. Following a faint path, they come upon an apparent fork, presenting two options. Somebody needs to make a decision, and if it is wrong the group could perish. The notional leader dithers: 'We could go left as that seems to feel the right direction, but there again, to the right takes us to higher ground where we can get a better sense of our bearings, although the sun suggests we might be going in the wrong direction altogether . . .' When someone steps forward and says with confidence, unequivocally, 'We should definitely go left', who do we follow? The 'certainty', of course, even if potentially ill-informed.

Listen to someone in the art world when asked their opinion about a painting. You won't hear them say: 'I am not sure. I *think* it is good, but there again I might be wrong – it really is hard to say.'

What you hear is pronouncement. 'This is a great painting', or 'This is a terrible painting'. Absolute certainty. And they can't be wrong because if they pronounce against the painting and the consensus is positive they will say, 'It might look good now but let's see in twenty-five years', and of course vice-versa if denouncing. We trust, and that is important, what with our inherent insecurities.

Now imagine that you are at that restaurant and you are undecided about your main course, wavering between the lamb and the salmon. You ask the server for advice. Would you prefer to hear 'Well, they are both very nice', or 'I would order the lamb', together with a quick explanation as to why?

Displaying confidence is crucial in the operation of a restaurant. Some restaurateurs insist on an ethos of 'we never say no', but I don't agree. There are certain requests for dishes not on the menu that can disrupt many a kitchen, and therefore need to be resisted, even if that's hard for a customer to understand. For many it has been the omelette that has the capacity to infuriate a chef; particularly an egg-white omelette. A server would be asked and would say 'let me check with the chef'. This is a 'lose-lose' situation, because even if they return to say 'That's fine', the chances are that the customer will either think or say: 'Well, of course it is, he's got eggs and a pan hasn't he – what's the prob-lem?' All said against a background of the customer thinking this is some judgement on their importance. My stricture is that the initial answer is, 'I am afraid we don't do egg-white omelettes – would you like to choose something else?' And if questioned then the answer is that it is house policy. Then of course the server can go and ask the chef and if agreed can return to the table and tell the customer that they have spoken to the chef and he is happy on this occasion to cook one. Now the customer feels important. We all want to feel that in life.

I like confidence, assertion and authority when dealing with problems, because there is less chance of escalation. One of my favourite learnings was when I worked at La Grenouille in Battersea with Michel Gautier, who, on encountering a problematical pair of men determined to cause trouble, didn't bother to engage and just lifted and removed the table, leaving the aggressors sitting exposed on their chairs and the centre of attention – they meekly left.

On another occasion, I asked a manager to speak to a loud group of men and request they be quieter. He duly did, but events turned nasty and I saw that one of the men was going around the tables shouting at other customers. After I had intervened I asked the manager what he had said and he confessed that he had tried to justify his action by saying other tables had complained, and thus one of the men was going around asking very aggressively, 'Was it *you* who complained about us?' As I explained, in this situation assertion is the only route: 'You are being too noisy and disturbing other guests and I need you to be quieter.'

One of my favourite memories of that very Parisian version of confidence – insouciance – was when I turned up for a late lunch at Café de Flore on Saint-Germain in the early Nineties. We had asked for a table and were about to be led to one when the manager paused, remembered there were new smoking laws and turned around with a sigh saying: '*Fumeur ou non-fumeur?*' We replied, 'No smoking', and were taken to the table. Oh, the classic French brasserie seating whereby you can't get into the banquette without completely pulling out the table, as he did, and I found that I was sitting 'cheek-by-jowl' with the tables either side, all four of whose occupants were smoking. I gestured to the manager in my best French sign language of outspread palms

and raised eyebrows whilst looking side to side, to which his response was to shrug his shoulders, raise his own eyebrows and take a 'No Smoking' sign from his pocket and place it on our table.

Brilliant.

# Talent

Like all businesses, talent is crucial to the success of a restaurant. But in restaurants we have two types of 'talent' – there's the staff, of course, but there's also the clientele. Here I want to talk about the latter.

Mario Gallati, manager of The Ivy in its original incarnation until 1945, and founder of the Caprice in its original incarnation in 1947, wrote in his memoirs about the importance of recognising and welcoming actors to the restaurant before they became famous. He counted James Mason and Laurence Harvey among his regulars, having welcomed them when they were still unknown and on the verge of fame.

This is a great skill. I often would say to my managers that if we were a Formula One racing team we would only be offering the seat to Damon Hill, whereas McLaren recognised the ability of Lewis Hamilton and gave him the car at the age of twenty-two. Sure, he must have made mistakes, but what dividends he paid by their recognition of his brilliance.

I am often perplexed by restaurant staff in high-profile restaurants who take little interest in the people walking through the door. For me, it is part of the joy of the job, and there are some who are superb – such as Kevin Lansdown, who joined us at Le Caprice in 1981 and is still going strong. His phenomenal powers of recognition and recall make him one of the greats.

I personally like to know EVERYTHING that is going on in the metropolis, and that includes all that is happening in football, for instance, even though I might have little interest in watching it. Knowledge enriches and excites, and I insist that every maître d'hôtel in our restaurants reads a broadsheet newspaper every day, cover to cover.

One short-lived reception manager I worked with just couldn't be bothered, until I drilled into him that anyone can blandly say 'Good evening, do you have a reservation?', but imagine walking into a restaurant to be greeted by name and how that makes you feel. We parted company fairly soon, but not before he tried out this game and the result was lavish commendation from a client who hadn't met him before, saying that he was brilliant – just because he knew him by name. It is a fundamental that no restaurateur should overlook or ignore. Remember that most of us would always go back to a restaurant where the food was only ok but the service wonderful, but never to a restaurant that have bad staff and service – however good the food.

It is also prudent for any restaurateur to recognise and respect the ancillary players in stardom – the agents, publicists, managers, etc., who are crucial to success but live in the shadow and rarely get the accolades and attention their client does. They need to be looked after, as indeed do the EAs and PAs who book the tables, as they can easily conspire against a restaurant that is foolish enough to disregard or be disdainful towards them.

This is not to say that the famous or up-and-coming and their entourages should get preferential treatment. In the restaurant business you should be nurturing your relationships with *all* customers. It's easy to pigeon-hole someone, and then it becomes immensely difficult to break away from the 'casting' we have. And yet there are so many examples of career changes that have transformed someone ordinary into a leader and innovator. One of my favourite artworks we commissioned for The Ivy was by Tom Phillips. Called 'The Professionals', it depicts ten of the 'Pillars of Modernism' – celebrated individuals who had had different careers before they found their true vocation and excelled as painters, writers, composers, etc. – 'Rousseau the Douanier' is a good example, but there are many whose earlier life would surprise . . .

Tom Phillips himself, sadly now deceased, was a good example of someone who defied pigeon-holing. His multitude of talents as painter,

sculptor, composer, librettist, writer, bookmaker, illustrator and much more unnerved many in the art world, who would have preferred him to stick to one style and medium so that they could compare and pronounce on new work as it appeared. He would have died richer if he had not resisted definition, but would he have died as happy and fulfilled?

# Do manners or clothes maketh the man?

I strongly disagree with the notion of a dress code being relevant or even effective in contemporary times. If I look at the question over the fifty years that I have been in hospitality, I can attest that the vast majority of serious problems I have experienced with customers have involved some troublemaker wearing a suit and a tie.

I have an internal trigger of apprehension when someone enters in a suit and then proceeds to dress down. There is, I am afraid, a ritual for a particular 'type'. The jacket comes off. (Savile Row would chide me for not using the proper term, 'coat' – a jacket is about sports or hacking – a suit has a coat. Hence an 'overcoat' or 'waistcoat' – ah! Suddenly it makes sense, doesn't it?) And as the 'coat' comes off the tie gets loosened, the top shirt button undone and the shirtsleeves are rolled up – just two cuffs' worth. This is the uniform of excessive drinking and loudness, and it puts me on red alert. So I can't understand the imposition of the need to wear either suit or tie.

Indeed, my 'dress code' heroes are those who have stood firm in the face of such narrow-minded diktats – such as the man who, despite being perfectly well dressed, was turned away from a London five-star hotel dining room because of the lack of jacket and tie. On being offered loan ones, he asked, 'So are you saying that as long as I wear this jacket and tie I can join my guests?' This was confirmed. Why is he a hero? Because he returned from the washrooms wearing absolutely nothing *but* the jacket and tie. The hotel hid behind an obscenity judgement in denying him entry, but oh how I admired him.

I realised that dress code was an issue soon after we opened Le Caprice in 1981, when a paparazzi photo revealed Andrew Lloyd Webber leaving the restaurant in a velvet jacket with an eccentric shirt and no tie and we received several letters of admonition (most peculiarly from haberdashers in Essex) upbraiding us for being prepared to condone such lapses in standards. I was shocked, but even more so when a few years later I was summoned to a table at Le Caprice by someone who described himself as a 'celebrity dentist'. Having beckoned me over, he gave a sideways look to the table next to him, raised his eyebrows, rolled his eyes and shook his head.

I didn't understand.

The couple next to him were two men dressed in good T-shirts and smart trousers. So I said to the head-shaker, 'Sorry, I don't understand what the problem is?'

'Look at them,' he hissed. 'Do I have to spell it out to you?'

'Well, yes.'

'They are wearing T-shirts! I can't possibly sit in a restaurant like this next to people wearing T-shirts.'

'Then you had better leave – now!'

And that's my attitude. I am often bemused by the number of people who assume that I will be an eagerly sympathetic ear when they bemoan the lack of a dress code in modern society and querulously lambast places such as the Royal Opera House for not imposing one. Of course, this assumed confederacy is because they only ever see me dressed formally in suit and tie, but they misunderstand that this how I feel most comfortable and myself, and not indicative of what I expect of them. It's a matter of self-expression, rather than convention, and because my business is also more easily conducted in my 'uniform'. Whilst there has been a relaxing of hospitality formality in both the service and uniforms, I do believe that it is easier for a customer to know who they are dealing with in the hierarchy, and therein lies the basis of my decision to always be formally dressed.

My response to the dress code advocates is simple. Fashion is cyclical; the more people dress down, the more it opens the door to those who wish to dress up to make an event special, and that can start a vogue within the cycle. The response is often, 'What about Glyndebourne?

Dress code works there.' Interestingly, this is not actually true, as there is no code at Glyndebourne. As the estimable proprietor Gus Christie says, it all comes down to whether you want to make the performers and yourself feel special. He's my other dress-code hero.

I don't believe there's been a continuing decline in so-called standards. If anything, perhaps the pendulum has begun to swing thanks to a thirst to step out of the sweatpants of the pandemic and embrace a desire to see and be seen. I found myself discussing the subject with the estimable and authoritative Timothy Everest – my tailor for thirty years – in his new outpost Grey Flannel, in Chiltern Street, now not only his retail operation but also his bespoke service. No one I know has a greater understanding and finger on the pulse of men's fashion than Timothy (notice that it is not women we are finding issues with regarding dress code – they generally seem to have an innate understanding of what is appropriate). Now, Timothy is convinced of a turn in the trend of 'couldn't care casual' to a very studied and personalised desire to be individual and innovative in our appearance. A wish not to conform to the norm at any level and be more expressive of our own character. And isn't that the nub of the matter? What we wear is surely reflective of how we are feeling, and no one should feel compelled to be anything other than ourselves. Certainly not forced into a uniform – whether it is the Meta chinos and T-shirt or the constraints of the suit – unless that's what *we* want.

I am far more interested in a person's manners than I am their clothing, and restaurant behaviour is one of the great revealers of character. When one of my daughters asked me how is it possible to ascertain whether to embark on a relationship with a potential partner – what are the tests? None better than spending an evening in a restaurant and observing how they treat the staff – any disdain, superiority, dismissiveness or condescension could be indicative of the way he will be treating you in time.

One of the greatest exponents of respect and egalitarianism, and one of the many reasons I love her so much, is Ruthie Rogers of The

River Cafe. Having tea with her and a granddaughter at The Wolseley I watched young Ivy, having ordered her cake, turn to her grandmother and say, 'Brown'. To which Ruthie nodded, congratulated her and continued talking.

'What was brown?' I asked, and was told that Ivy had been taught that she could never order anything in a restaurant unless she could then say what colour the waiter's eyes were. It is something we can all learn from.

We might have (just about) moved on from the days of the clicking of fingers and the utter disdain with which some restaurant clients treat staff, but it has yet to be eradicated. I find it hard to fathom what people hope to achieve with their contemptuous treatment of fellow human beings. It is irrational to antagonise someone who has such power over your enjoyment and indeed what you are about to put into your mouth. Mercifully, we have done away with the 'revenge actions' of waiting staff, but restaurant critic AA Gill was probably not wrong in asserting that he was sure that he ingested more spittle than any of his colleagues! Indeed, when I was starting out in the industry, a complaining customer might arrive home only to discover sauce on the back of their jacket, or having suffered in other ways at the hands of the 'old timer' nastiness. For instance, a complaint of a plate being cold would result in a replacement being 'grilled' under the salamander and then placed in front of the complainant much too close to them, with the advice, 'careful the plate is hot', which would go unheeded and the client would sear their fingers.

Generally, there is a greater mutual respect and understanding nowadays. I remember optimistically declaring post-pandemic that I hoped customers would learn to respect staff more, and in turn that restaurants and their staff would respect the customers more. Sadly, it hasn't quite turned out that way; instead, the Brexit-induced paucity of sufficient numbers of good staff has meant that shoddier service is often offered, whilst prices have risen exponentially.

Unfortunately, the prevailing notion that 'The customer is always right' has too frequently been proven a falsehood. I am happy to expound on tolerance and understanding, and I even sympathise with the notion that 'The customer is right – until proven wrong', as so many restaurateurs often like to believe. However, it is ultimately potentially too adversarial and confrontational for my liking. I like to think the best of everyone, but as soon as the line is crossed I am rather categoric and forthright in my reactions. The truth is, once they've earned my trust, I always take the side of the staff.

I once received a call from The Wolseley saying that there was a big problem with a regular client who was a financial advisor and accountant to many a famous star. This is always dangerous, because whilst 'principals' may possess good principles, the entourage often likes to wield the power of association and therein we find the source of most fights. This man, call him Stephen, had created a real stink about the table he had been allocated (remember the aphorism 'Those who care, don't count – those who count, don't care') and after this bad start was complaining about everything and everyone. On my walk back to the restaurant the manager filled me in over the phone on the details and how Stephen had threatened them all with losing their jobs – standard bullying tactics. As I stepped through the door he was sitting at the front in reception, anticipating my arrival, and on seeing me smugly smiled at the manager and colleagues at the desk, who looked apprehensive. And as he rose to make his complaint, I told him to 'Get out now'.

He was shocked. 'Are you not going to hear my account?' he said.

'No. I have heard from the staff what happened and I trust them, whereas I don't trust you.'

'But they were rude to me!'

I explained that the moment I am told that a member of staff was allegedly 'rude' is when I end the discussion, because I have learnt empirically, with 99 per cent accuracy, that it just isn't the case. 'Were they really "rude" or did they just tell you something you didn't want to hear? – which is, I suspect, the truth of the matter.'

In brief, if you can't trust your staff and colleagues then you are working with the wrong people.

I'll give the final word on the matter to outspoken chef/writer/TV personality Anthony Bourdain, who said in an interview:

*'The worst customer on the Earth is the customer who's decided beforehand they're already miserable the minute they walk in the door and they've decided that they're going to feel better if they bully, speak condescendingly to or mistreat floor staff. This is an unforgiveable act to me. If we go out to lunch together and you're rude to your waiter and treat them like a piece of shit, talk down to them or blame them for the kitchen's mistakes – our relationship is dead and will always be dead.'*

Quite.

Now it's time to share with you one of the many staff tools that we developed over the years when it comes to dealing with rowdy behaviour.

Imagine you are in, say, a party of six and the service starts to be rather over-attentive, then the chances are you are being too loud. Loudness, shouting and excessive laughter are normally the result of anecdotes, and I am afraid it is the anecdote that dominates when a group has nothing to say to each other, surmise, exchange, discuss or have any real conversation about. And it is important to understand that within the domain of contemporary restaurants rarely paying any attention to their acoustics until it is too late to remedy, it is only too easy for the decibel levels of a restaurant to be doubled by one loud anecdote-led table. The acoustics of too many contemporary restaurants exacerbate these problems and I am always very alert to the intrinsic and insidious effect that a harsh acoustic environment can have on an experience.

If I am around that evening, you will see far too much of me and your server, because as there is an ever-increasing level of shouting and laughter, so we will be interceding. Not in the way of the omnipresent waiter in Harold Pinter's play *Celebration*, but by checking just a bit too much that 'everything is alright'. And the more observant source of the noise will notice that those interventions increase the louder you are and how they are particularly prevalent just as punchlines are about to be delivered. And if you experience the irritating and distracting feeling of someone kicking your chair as you shout louder, then be sure it is me or a manager purposely doing it. The food will arrive surprisingly quickly as well, and that's no coincidence as we know that it is harder to talk with your mouth full and that the hard drinkers are invariably greedy and can't refrain from eating.

I am afraid restaurants have to be about control, and it is the restaurateur who sets the guidelines – if they are any good. If a table is disturbing everyone in the room then I would rather upset six people than have 150 others upset by them. That's the skill – knowing who to bring into the restaurant and how to marshal them. And in the event that the defences are breached by the inappropriately behaved, knowing how to assert control and authority over them. Should a restaurateur fail to assert the house standards of behaviour, their precious domain will fail.

It was for this reason that in December, 'Party Month', across all our restaurants we would only take reservations of up to four people unless we knew them. And when I say 'know' them, I mean well enough that if we have cause to ask the group to 'moderate' then they will, without argument or confrontation.

As a postscript on the way that I personally dress: I came to realise what the expectation is of me when one Saturday I came through the door of The Wolseley to drop something off at Reception, but dressed in casual clothes. At that moment a waiter came out of the bar and on seeing me stopped in his tracks and promptly dropped the plates he was carrying, because of the shock of seeing me out of a suit.

# Defensiveness

Defensiveness is ultimately a tactic destined for failure. How frustrating is it when someone will not concede that they have made a mistake, trying instead to justify their actions? I am often surprised by just how hard people fight to cover their shortcomings, rather than the much more disarming admission. After all, normally those who have found fault just need it to be acknowledged and learned from – it's not about recrimination or punishment.

Restaurants are, sadly, often built around defensiveness, and when staff fail there is no better way of riling me than saying, 'I was doing the best I could.' That is rarely true and is usually an attempt to shift responsibility. Why on earth isn't it possible to admit, agree and spend more time rectifying the issue rather than denying it?

I had an Ivy sous chef who was incapable of conceding an error. Typical was the day when I was in the kitchen and a waiter came down with a returned steak. 'What's wrong with it?' barked Greg, to which the reply came, 'Customer says it is inedible', to which Greg acted out the usual chef reaction – to prod the steak (assessing if it was cooked properly and its tenderness). 'Don't prod it,' I tell him, 'try a piece.' And so he did and then proceeded to chew, and chew, and chew. And chew, and chew, and chew until I said, 'Well?' and with great difficulty he swallowed the piece, saying 'I wouldn't say it was inedible . . .'

And through my gritted teeth of frustration I said, 'But is it *right?*'

'No,' he conceded, finally.

And that's the point. It shouldn't be about semantics. Is it right?

I still smile when I think of a restaurant view by Craig Brown in the late Eighties of a place in Twickenham. Craig is one of the great journalists, with prolific writings, pastiches and observations from *Private*

*Eye* to *The Times*. As I remember it, he had an 8.30 p.m. booking and come 9.45 p.m. still hadn't received any food. He asked for the manager, saying to tell him that they had been waiting an hour and a quarter for their food. The manager soon appeared, asking, 'Are you the people saying you have been waiting seventy-five minutes for your food? Well, we have an electronic ordering system so I can show you that in fact you were slow to order, at 8.57 p.m., and have therefore only been waiting forty-eight minutes,' he said triumphantly. Which elicited Craig's response: 'Isn't that still a rather long time?'

In the attempt to guard against being perceived in any way as failing, we ultimately fail. If, instead, we admit a problem, fault or failing, the effect tends to be disarming. When it comes to customer complaints, I have found the best way to deal with them, if food, is to insist that the chef comes onto the floor to speak to the customer. Chefs don't like this, understandably, and try their hardest to obviate the need, but when they do it is so effective. If I or a manager goes to apologise or explain, the customer often feels that they are just being fobbed off or indulged, but the appearance of the chef in his toque (tall hat) suddenly humanises the situation. Apologising and explaining normally has the customer empathising rather than feeling frustrated.

Of course, we have all suffered at the hands of some pompous know-it-all who feels the need to dispense their opinion, even when not wanted. I know it is painful but I am going to advise, even here, listening and not getting exasperated. It is just possible that sometimes they will have a useful point buried amidst the pontifications and bluster – however irritating listening to it can be. A good example for me was a certain David Damant, who I found excruciatingly painful to be around, exacerbated by us being members of the same club – although, by not being a particularly regular club attender myself meant I was spared him other than as a customer.

In he would come with his opinions. He would complain that the soup wasn't hot enough, the red wine too warm, the white wine too cold (on which subject he was actually right, but wasn't prepared to countenance that 99 per cent of other customers do like their white wine cold). My lesson from him came one evening at The Ivy.

'Jeremy,' he began, 'you really must convince your staff that this is a good restaurant.'

What on earth was he on about?

'Well,' he explained, 'when I arrive the door to my taxi is opened by Sean who welcomes me and says "Enjoy your meal". After I drop off my coat the attendant says she hopes I will enjoy my dinner, as does the maître d'hôtel as he asks the assistant to seat me, who in turn says, "Enjoy your evening", and then the manager repeats the same as he takes my order. Even the person who delivers the food says "Enjoy". By now I would be justified in thinking that your staff are not confident that I will actually enjoy and are getting a bit pleading in the exhortation to enjoy, and I wonder if there is something I should know.'

He was, annoyingly, absolutely right. I was oblivious to the repetition because I would be treated differently when I came to eat. I had already discovered that I needed to look afresh at the physical aspects of the room and public areas, as if through the eyes of somebody scrutinising them for the first time, but the service that I thought was accomplished actually was looking rather amateurish.

And so I learned that however intimate and close you are to your business, there are things you don't see that others do.

# The power of positivity

One of the best lessons I learned about leadership comes from a story related by the late artist Tom Phillips (he of 'The Professionals' artwork at The Ivy). How I loved Tom, despite him being not a little curmudgeonly. He was often described – and loathed the description – as the true 'Renaissance Man', on account of the wide extent of the disciplines he embraced as an artist, musician, writer and collector. Now I often think the true calibre of a man or woman is ascertained by the quality of funeral they are given – especially if partially planned by the deceased. They can control the music and order of service, but they can't determine what is said. Amongst others, Tom was lucky enough to have Simon Callow deliver a perfect eulogy that captured the depth of him – I suppose it is fair comment that we make our own luck.

*The Independent – portrait of Jeremy King*

Tom was probably the most learned, intelligent, well-read and brilliant person I have ever met, but this is just one simple story from his rich life, which concerned his love and pursuit of African art. He had assembled the greatest collection of 'gold weights' in the world and was one of the most revered authorities on African art generally, as exemplified by his defining exhibition at the Royal Academy.

Every year Tom and a group of enthusiasts, experts and collectors would visit sites in Africa led by a tour organiser. I think there were normally eight travellers and the only part that Tom dreaded was selecting which sites to visit. The pre-tour meeting would be defined by arguments, rancour and dispute, because the decisions as to where the group should visit were controversial and inflammatory – destined to cause dissent. That is, until the leader changed everything one year.

He explained that he was proposing twenty site options, as usual, and that there would only be time to visit at best twelve. Instead of discussion turning into argument there would be a simple rule: if one, just one, of the party voted for a site then it would be included – and if necessary all twenty sites would be visited – albeit in a rushed and unsatisfactory way. And if anyone criticised the nominee in any way, or queried why they wanted that site, they would be thrown off the trip. The leader had cleverly awarded the individual power over the group. The power of positivity would trump negativity.

The result? The group only visited nine sites that year and the visits were more effective and satisfactory than ever. The politics were removed and each individual examined their motivation before making their recommendation, knowing that if they were only trying to be selfish or controversial the group would have to suffer in silent judgement. There would be no pleasure in the win for win's sake. I have remained an advocate of the power of positivity ever since, and believe a reason to do something must hold the edge over the motivation not to.

This was encapsulated for me in a conversation I had with a black cab driver sitting outside The Ritz, presumably waiting for a ride to the airport. I was late for an appointment and it was beginning to rain, so

I asked him if he would be terribly upset if I only asked him to take me to the top of Berkeley Square – probably a three-minute ride. 'Jump in, mate, and let's get you there.'

Once in I apologised again for depriving him of his pole position on the taxi rank.

'Don't worry at all, I have a simple philosophy that my next job could be the best of my working life. It might be a job to Birmingham, or I get a great racing tip or even meet my future wife. No such thing as a bad job.'

I have taken a great deal from that philosophy.

# Celebration

On the occasion of Ed Victor's sixtieth birthday, in September 1999, we were gathered at the house of Richard and Ruthie Rogers for the celebratory dinner – a venue that I believe has seen more joyful celebrations per square foot than any other private home. I find myself sat next to Ruthie and opposite Harold Pinter when Harold suddenly announced:

'I have written a play.'

'As you do,' I said, cheekily.

He ignored me. 'It's set in a restaurant.'

Ruthie and I wanted to know more, but no further information was forthcoming so we let it drop. What we didn't realise at the time was that the play would be premiered only six months later.

So early in March 2000, into Le Caprice post-theatre comes a group including the film producer Eric Fellner and Alan Yentob, then Director of Drama, Entertainment and Children's Programmes at the BBC. When I went over to say hello they pointed at me and started laughing, saying, 'There he goes – just like that!' Seeing my confusion, they explained that they had been to a preview of Harold Pinter's new play, *Celebration*, at The Almeida and it was set in a restaurant and the restaurateur had all my mannerisms and gestures down pat. 'What you just did with your hands on the back of the chair happens in the play. Harold must have been studying you.'

That didn't sound good.

I then went to The Ivy to see the post-theatre clientele there and I found Harold and Antonia ensconced at their usual table. As I walked up to them Harold appeared a little uncomfortable and Antonia was smiling mischievously.

'Did it go well this evening?' I asked.

'Ah yes,' Harold said, looking at Antonia, 'we have just come from The Almeida. I have written a play.'

'Yes, indeed – and directed as well – you told Ruthie and me about it at Ed's birthday. I'm coming to the opening on Thursday.'

'You are?' he said, again looking uncomfortably at Antonia. 'Listen,' followed by a long 'Pinteresque' pause, 'I wouldn't want you to think that this play is based on any actual restaurant.'

'Of course not.'

'And (another long pause), I wouldn't want you to think that any character in it was based on any particular person.'

'Of course not. That would be somewhat unprofessional, wouldn't it?'

'Yes, it would.'

I can't be sure, but I am convinced I saw a wince as he said that, then he abruptly finished the conversation with, 'Good. We've got that straight then.'

I didn't know what to expect as I approached The Almeida for the press night – that is, until I was outside and ran into Hilton McRae, the husband of Lindsay Duncan, who was the lead actress in the production.

'Do yourself a favour, Jeremy, turn around and go home,' he said firmly. 'You don't want to be here tonight.'

I stayed. When the play started and Thomas Wheatley, playing the restaurateur, came on stage I heard my voice, and saw my mannerisms and even my looks. Indeed, my old chef Charles Fontaine, who was sitting in the circle to see his friend Keith Allen, thought it *was* me. AA Gill wrote subsequently, 'At that moment Jeremy King learned what it was like to be the Queen at the theatre when someone mentions the Royal Family or swears – half the theatre turned to look at him.'

I was mortified. I kept my wits about me enough to phone through to The Ivy, where Harold and Antonia were going afterwards, and asked Mitchell, the general manager, to put a glass of gherkins on the table: a reference to a scene in the play when the restaurateur goes into a reverie about how significant they are in his life. And having done so, I avoided the audience and raced home to reflect.

I was deeply hurt because I couldn't be sure if I was being ridiculed or 'celebrated'. But I resolved not to comment to the press and their enquiries, nor make any comment, get annoyed, appear hurt – just stay silent.

And the dividend that decision paid me was that, not too long later, I was asked out of the blue by Susanna Gross whether I was still playing bridge. Susan was an international bridge player and bridge journalist, who was a friend. She went on to explain that Harold and Antonia would like me to join the three of them for dinner and bridge.

Unexpected.

Soon after I arrived for the evening at Harold and Antonia's home in Campden Hill Square I realised that Antonia and Susanna had disappeared, leaving Harold and me together. Harold couldn't have been more generous in apologising for any discomfort I had felt at *Celebration* and wanted to reassure me that the portrayal was not literal but affectionate and purely a device. This consolidated a friendship. The bridge evenings continued, and with them a collection of memories that I treasure and cherish.

Later still, Harold's friend, the American playwright and screenwriter David Mamet was so tickled by the gherkin story that he sent me a small box he had commissioned, with a single ceramic gherkin in as a commemoration.

There is a coda to this tale, another perception lesson. This occurred a few years later in 2005 when theatre impresario and producer Nick Allott came into The Wolseley and announced:

'I have just seen you! It was great. When are you going?'

He had seen the first of three evenings at The Albery (now the Noël Coward Theatre), honouring the now sick and absent Harold after his award of the Nobel Prize in Literature. It included *Celebration* as one of the works in a rehearsed reading.

'I'm not. Too painful.'

'Oh, you must, you'll love it,' and not wanting to take no for an answer he insisted on setting up the ticket for me.

I arrived with an even greater apprehension than I had done at The Almeida, which was heightened as Antonia looked around from her seat in front to find me and declared it was 'my play'. And yet, that evening, remarkably, I witnessed an entirely different play to that at The Almeida and soon was enveloped by the dulcet tones of Charles Dance, who had a completely different take on the role of the restaurateur. Gone was the

*Cast of* Celebration *revival at Duke of York's*

obsequious and weak character, instead, here was an intelligent, slightly disdainful and even supercilious version – I loved it.

I try to stay open-minded about everything in life, and if anything I discovered the importance of that philosophy that evening. Nevertheless, I couldn't bring myself to attend the after-party Antonia was hosting at Sheekey's – I guess I will always be at heart introverted and shy – but at that point I did allow myself a little pride.

# Harold Pinter

*'The half of Harold that is not Beckett, is Hemingway.'* Antonia Fraser

When I received the call from Susanna Gross, on Christmas Day 2008, that Harold had died, I felt I had lost my father. The intensity of my emotion caught me by surprise, and the tears flowed as I cooked Christmas lunch for the children. Later that day I walked in a daze around Hyde Park trying to reconcile myself to why I felt so bereft – after all, he had not always been easy and I had often been on the receiving end of his frustration or anger.

My first real encounter with the wrath of Harold was an evening in 1984, soon after his arrival, with Antonia Fraser, at Le Caprice. They were an hour early for their reservation, their favourite table was not yet vacant and this seemed to trouble Harold inordinately. I asked what had occasioned the change of plan and Antonia said they had left a play at the interval. I knew that Harold steadfastly endured to the end the work of contemporary writers, even if he didn't like what he saw, so I assumed this must have been an old play. I was wrong; the work that he had been so deeply offended by was Michael Hastings' *Tom & Viv*, a play about T. S. Eliot's ill-fated marriage to Vivienne Haigh-Wood. Pinter was understandably upset, and I could only admire his principled anger, but at the same time it was Antonia, the staff and me who were enduring the ire. The risk-taker in me was roused, and out of frustration with being delivered another growl I foolishly said: 'Oh come on – it is not as if the play was Hal & Toni . . .'

I thought he was going to punch me, but as he rose a restraining hand from Antonia, together with her laughter, rescued me and avoided the fracas. All credit to him allowing the restraint – and more indication of the love of and trust in his wife.

She was a wonderful foil for him and over the years often inter-ceded on my behalf and that of many others.

For all it could cause ructions, I respected Harold's single-minded concentration on his preoccupations. I recall one evening in 1995 when, on seeing me, he dispensed with the courtesy of 'hello' and went straight to:

'Jeremy. Have you seen my new play yet?'

'I didn't think you had one on?' I said. He conceded it wasn't his play but Ronald Harwood's *Taking Sides*, which he was directing.

'I haven't yet, I am afraid.'

'Why not?'

'I haven't had a chance.'

'Why not?'

Antonia tried to help. 'You might remember, Harold, that Jeremy and Debra have just had their third child.'

'What's that got to do with it? What are you talking about?'

It was with that effective admonition in the back of my mind when later that year I took the first opportunity possible to go and see Harold perform in his own play, *The Hothouse*, at The Comedy Theatre (later renamed the Harold Pinter Theatre). There I found myself sitting a few seats away from Salman Rushdie. In the interval we shared our mutual incomprehension about the play.

'What will you say to him?' Salman asked.

'Nothing,' I replied.

'You have to say something,' he exclaimed.

'No, I don't . . . you being here obviates the need for me to go backstage.'

'Wish me luck. Reminds me of the time at The Ivy when I fluffed my lines after seeing Harold's production of *Oleanna* – you were there, in fact. Antonia and I had come over from the theatre and were chat-ting away at the table when Harold joined us and then got angry because he felt left out.'

I interjected: 'That was your fault for sitting in between the two of them.'

'Yes, and I made matters worse because I continued to talk to Antonia after he arrived; that is, until I felt a dark cloud above us and realised that Harold was not happy. I knew what to do and said to him: "Harold, did I neglect to tell you that tonight was one of the best effing directed plays I have ever seen?"'

'Yes, you did.'

'And there was silence only punctuated by Harold's stare . . . And I realised I had to continue. "Harold, tonight was one of the best effing directed plays I have ever seen."'

'That's better.'

Demanding, yes, but also admirably frank. Too many of us brood about perceived slights, rudeness and lack of respect. If we were all as candid as Harold was there would be far less tension in the air.

Sometimes I would get myself into trouble answering his questions. Like the time when, over dinner, he asked me what I was reading and I stumbled into the wrong answer by saying that I was reading *In the Heat of the Day* by Elizabeth Bowen – did he know it?

'DO I KNOW IT? Of course I bloody do – I wrote probably my best screenplay based on it!'

Now I was nervous, and I potentially dug a greater hole by saying, 'Then I can only imagine it was never produced . . .'

'YES IT WAS!'

'I know all your film screenplays and that is not one of them.'

And then, on reflection, he conceded that it was actually made for TV.

'That would explain it – I rarely watch TV.' Phew.

Thinking that I had avoided the faux pas, I then found myself mired by subsequently answering Antonia's question: 'Are you reading anything else?' by telling her that I was re-reading Anthony Powell's *A Dance to the Music of Time*, and had she?

'He was my uncle.'

Harold would continue to test my navigation of tricky questions and moments. In the middle of bridge one evening in 2005, partnering with Susanna, Harold said:

'I have found a poem I wrote – never published. Would you like to hear it?'

Well, if that's not the biggest rhetorical question ever then I don't know what is. And although Antonia asked whether it was a good idea – she mentioned the previous audience was not really enthusiastic – we eagerly nodded and Harold prepared himself to recite. Here is the poem in its entirety.

> *Breasts, Bottom, Thighs, the whole palaver*
> *I raise my hat to my uncensored sister*
> *Who shone the light of love on those about her*
> *Who lusted longest on her black suspender*
>
> (HP 1973 – rediscovered 2005)

'What do you think?' Harold asked.

What can you dare to say? My solution was to ask whether it had a title and, on discovering that it didn't, to opine that such an important poem deserved a title and should we discuss it? Susanna kicked me under the table because she knew the spotlight would now be on her.

On another occasion, once again playing bridge, the conversation turned to the subject of failure. 'No matter,' I remarked, 'try again, fail again, fail better.' Harold seemed startled and asked me how I knew that quotation.

'Tom Phillips included it in his depiction of Beckett watching a rehearsal of *Waiting for Godot*.'

The next question felt more accusatory: 'So it was *you* that beat me to it?'

'Not me, my copy came from the artist.' Harold explained that he had tried to buy a copy at auction and was upset that he indeed had failed. But he didn't have to try again, because a few weeks later I was able to witness the pure joy on his face to receive Tom's last personal copy of said lithograph.

While he could be easily considered difficult and cantankerous, it would not be a fair assessment to define Harold in those terms. My

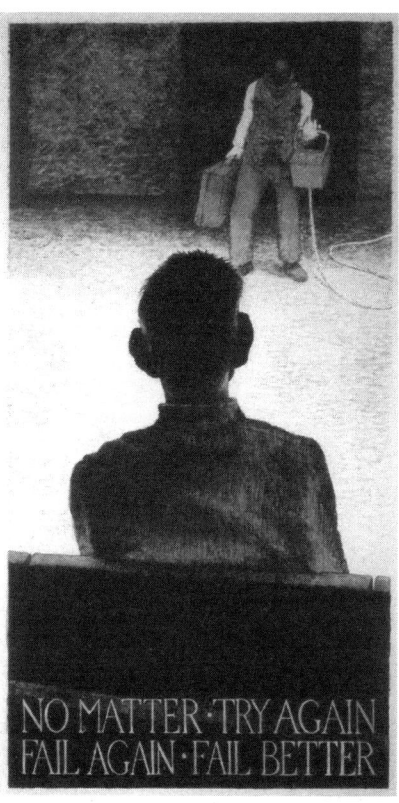

own attraction and fondness for him centred on his straightforward, unbridled honesty combined with his egalitarian principles and passionate hatred of bullies (how he would have railed against the American elections of 2016 and 2024). It was a privilege to be in the orbit of such a stellar mind and I realise every day how much I miss him and indeed how much the world needs more principled torchbearers.

On Christmas Day 2008, I dropped a note through Antonia's door asking whether I could help. She replied, 'Never ask unless you mean it – yes please.' So The Wolseley catered the small wake that followed one of the most emotional experiences of my life. Tom Stoppard summed up the feeling at the funeral in Kensal Green Cemetery – with readings poignantly delivered by Michael Gambon, Penelope Wilton, Matthew Burton and others – when he said, 'You could cut the grief with a knife.'

When Antonia approached the grave and softly recited, 'Now cracks a noble heart. Goodnight, sweet prince, and flights of angels sing thee to thy rest,' I couldn't, nor wanted to, stem the tears.

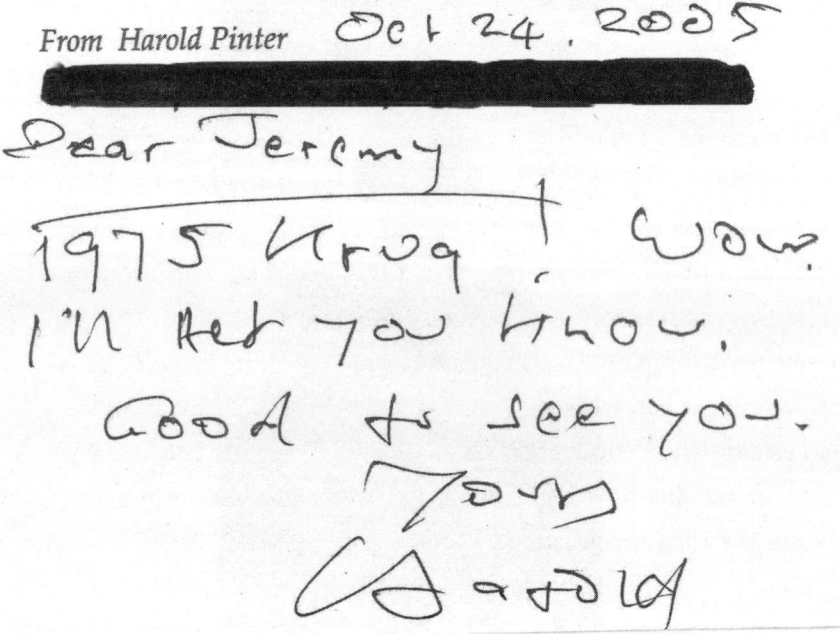

*From Harold Pinter* Oct 24, 2005

Dear Jeremy

1975 Krug! Wow.
I'll let you know.
Good to see you.
Tom
Harold

# Alone is not lonely

Jean-Paul Sartre said, 'If you're lonely when you are alone, you're in bad company.' Indeed, I relish being by myself – particularly when it comes to dining. In truth, I find it the only way to properly enjoy a starry Michelin experience, as so often those types of restaurants can conspire against conversation and conviviality. Nubar Gulbenkian, the great Armenian-Englishman who lived above the old Caprice, once said, 'The best dining companion is a good head waiter.' (He was not only wealthy but eccentric and was so taken by the London taxis that he converted one for his own use – something I tried to buy in 1993 but was outbid on. He famously remarked: 'It can turn on a sixpence – whatever that is!')

I'm aware that there is a stigma around eating alone, and yet nothing could be farther from the truth. Inevitably we are all at some point 'stood up' for lunch or dinner because of misunderstandings or miscommunications, and many people feel a sense of shame to be the one left alone at a table. The instinct is to hurriedly ask for the bill and scurry away, and this is where I step in and implore the 'victim' to stay – unless they genuinely need to recover the time – saying: 'You still need to eat. Stay as my guest, I will get you a paper and you can relax, or catch up on your messages and emails and enjoy the luxury of your own company. The problem is that *you* think that the restaurant is looking at you with pity, whereas in truth it is with admiration. It is so elegant and confident to eat alone and they envy you.'

I remember how impressed I was, during a visit in the early Eighties to the then much-lauded Jacques Cagna restaurant in St Germain, Paris, by an indomitable grand dame of another era sitting alone at the table next to mine. She quietly ate her meal accompanied by sips of her wonderful Salon le Mesnil Champagne from a bottle by one of the all-time coveted *millesimes*, but which she had barely troubled; it turned out she was an Italian countess. When the eponymous chef came from the kitchen he bowed to her and enquired: 'Did you enjoy your meal, Comtessa?' and I watched him squirm as she made her observations with quiet dignity, criticising several elements and particularly the spinach. She was the star of the room, indubitably, and I vowed from that moment I would always enjoy solo dining and also give appropriate feedback when asked, rather than the platitudes too often used instead of the truth. While not always comfortable to receive, honest feedback is normally of much greater generosity to the restaurateur.

Being alone is more likely to encourage companionship than ostracisation and there is no doubt that is a good thing. However, I still yearn sometimes to be alone, but for years I was too polite to safeguard that solitude – that is until I witnessed the Master, the actor Edward Fox, showing just how. He had come into Le Caprice after a performance, I think in *The Admirable Crichton* in the 1980s, having booked in solo, and was sitting at a prominent table. As I walked down the bar I overheard two journalists discussing him:

'Isn't that Edward Fox by himself?'

'Yes, do you know him?'

'Yes, I do a bit,' was the reply, 'I think I will just say hello.'

And so with me trailing him on red alert I followed the man to the table.

The journalist said hello, introduced himself and reached to pull out a chair, saying: 'Mind if I join you?' To which most people would say with a resigned tone, 'Of course.' But not the Master, whose reply was accompanied with a raised hand:

'I am dining alone this evening.'

There was no need for my intervention.

For an illustration of the advantages of solo dining, one need look no further than to any restaurant on Valentine's Day.

The thing that must be understood is that Valentine's night is the worst evening to be in a restaurant – especially as a couple. Not every couple, but I am afraid that many are there under duress or obligation. There is too often the expectation, pressure, discomfort and the sad but steady realisation of unhappiness. Why? Because the average pair on Valentine's night tends to be a couple with young children and a mixed expectation. (It remains predominately heterosexual for some reason – perhaps because the queer community recognises the artifice of it?)

Although society changes have altered this, for many years the first defining feature of Valentine's Day was how early the phone started ringing in the morning. Most of these inordinately early calls were coming from husbands who had forgotten it was 'The Day' in the first place, and who had departed for work after a loaded question having been asked by their partner about the evening, with the sudden realisation that no booking had been made, nor flowers bought, or card signed, or chocolates purchased. I actually use these calls as a training tool, because it defines a restaurant how the reception staff respond. Whilst there is normally no chance at all of fulfilling the request, there is nothing to be gained by humiliating the caller with the response. After taking so many futile calls the temptation to laugh, snort, howl, be incredulous or ask whether they are kidding is manifest. But that is unacceptable and we need to let the desperate begging be thwarted kindly and sympathetically.

For those who have found a reservation, what is the reality? For my own part, I try to restrict the parties of two to an absolute minimum on this night because there is nothing worse than the average Valentines' table plan. Extra tables of two inserted to compensate for the number of 'four-tops' that will be underfilled. Generally, the couple find themselves in a line of twos almost closer to their neighbour than their loved one (have you noticed how tables of two are getting longer but narrower so that all the 'sharing plates' can be accommodated without the table occupying too much space?). It is so difficult to be intimate when your silent co-diners can hear your every word. And the pressure is building.

Our couple haven't been out for dinner alone for some time now – probably for a year exactly! The demands of work and children mean that the rare dinner opportunities are with friends so they haven't sat across the table and looked each other in a while. And what are they going to say to each other? The couple to one side might be silent but on the other side there are kisses, held hands, maybe even an offered ring with laughter and chatter and general love hubbub.

The pressure is building. This is because on Valentine's night it is unacceptable to talk about the kids, work, the house, family or friends – the only topic really acceptable is them, and frankly, from my observations, an unappreciated wife, mother, partner, facilitator, listener and much more is goading the situation by their understandable need for: 'Tell me you love me.' I am afraid this becomes too much for many men and they consequently resort to their best solution – they start a row. Inevitably this leads to a frustrated outburst from the ill-treated partner about the state of the relationship and the man seizes upon this to justify his behaviour. There might be a continuing row, but more likely silence ensues. There might be a sudden departure, even a thrown glass, and I have seen wedding rings jettisoned, faces slapped and of course even earlier in this cycle arranged Champagne for proposal celebrations hastily cancelled.

All of this as part of an evening that truly is the worst for atmosphere in any restaurant.

It's worth saying again: alone is not lonely.

# Inspiration

When asked what is the most influential restaurant experience I have experienced, my answer is that there are three.

First, being taken by Allan Scott, the screenwriter and former head of Macallan whisky, to a new restaurant in South Kensington in 1983 called Hilaire. The chef was Simon Hopkinson, and the food was exemplary, but the moment it became exemplary was when I ordered cheese – I think it was Double Gloucester. On arrival I gasped with surprise because instead of the batons of cheese, grapes, nuts, chutney, carved tomato, etc., that were the norm at the time, all there was on the plate was a simple but generous slice of cheese – with nothing else except some bread and a single type of biscuit on the side. This was breathtaking and exhilarating, as it paved the way for a simplicity that was also pioneered by Simon's contemporaries Alastair Little and Rowley Leigh.

It was Alastair who provided the second revelation when, at his eponymous restaurant in Soho, I ordered the rather prosaic-sounding

'Tomatoes on Toast'. What could he possibly do with that which would justify the hype he was enjoying? Well, I was blown away again. The sweetest, firmest, sautéed cherry tomatoes – which truly tasted as tomatoes once had – were presented cascading off a perfectly toasted slice of granary bread dripping in rich olive oil and topped with pepper and sea salt. The generosity, the love and the flavours were previously not experienced back then in 1985.

But the third and most impressive dish was that which I was served at Jonathan Waxman's restaurant JAMS in New York City, also in 1985.

I had heard about this chef who, along with Alice Waters (with whom he had worked at her legendary restaurant, Chez Panisse), was transforming American restaurants with his ingredients-led 'Californian cuisine'. He had been cooking at Michael's restaurant, co-founded with Michael McCarty, in Santa Monica, and now he was bringing his style of food to New York.

I was already impressed with the simplicity of the restaurant, with its white walls, defined with American oak and beautifully lit modern art before the main course arrived. It was listed as corn-fed chicken from a specific farm in upstate New York, and served with French fries. And just as with Hilaire, that's what arrived. Who does that? Names

the source of the chicken and how it is reared. It was sublime on every level and probably has to win the accolade of greatest dish for me. Jonathan ended up being not only a great friend but also an advisor, and he still has the best contemporary chicken dish at his Lower West Side restaurant Barbuto: 'Pollo al Forno with salsa verde'.

Nowadays the dishes that tend to inspire me are often found at The River Cafe, where again ingredients, simplicity, love, care and attention reign supreme and most of my best culinary and social experiences

*With Ruthie, Rose and Richard*

have taken place. There are too many to single out, whether birthdays for my kids, my wife Lauren or me, or indeed Ruthie and Richard, but the one that really makes me smile is taking my daughter Hannah there for lunch when she was two – in 1993 – at the original café, and never has a dining companion been better nor happier.

It fuels my belief that the best restaurants are those that appeal across all age groups. To be the catalyst for happy memories is a privilege.

# Part 3: 2000s, The Wolseley

# Confidence

As the millennium approached, Chris and I were the proud owners of three successful London restaurants – Le Caprice, The Ivy and J. Sheekey – which we ran under the business name of Caprice Holdings Ltd. We were in the fortunate position, rarely achievable these days, of being 100 per cent owners of our business and therefore entirely independent of any shareholder opinion. However, there were fears of an impending global financial meltdown, and with Chris only recently recovered from a life-threatening leukaemia diagnosis, when we were approached in 1998 by Luke Johnson, a notorious 'restaur-preneur' who enjoyed great success with the Pizza Express and Belgo Groups, to sell the group, we felt it prudent to accept.

Then, in 2000, we stepped away from the restaurants. We understood that our future was too inextricably bound up with the success of Luke's company, and that wasn't working out. And we were also experiencing the shock of somebody trying to tell us what to do.

My intention was to move into the world of hotels. But my attempts to do so were thwarted by being outmuscled by cash-rich groups. It was when I remonstrated with my agent that we were failing to find a hotel that he suggested I do another restaurant in the interim. What he had in mind was the recently failed China House restaurant on Piccadilly, in the old Barclays Bank and previous Wolseley car showroom building.

I was less than enthusiastic, saying that I'd never seen an old bank successfully transform into a restaurant. But he encouraged me to at least go and have a look. When I did, I realised the potential and immediately took Chris to see it.

'Wouldn't this work perfectly as the Grand Café you've always dreamed of opening?' he asked.

'That's just what I was thinking.'

Nine months later, The Wolseley was born.

Someone who helped me through the hurdles and pitfalls of opening The Wolseley was Charles Saatchi, founder of the global advertising agency, who in a virtuoso 'talking to' helped me move from being a 'people pleaser' to a 'pleaser of people'. There is a difference.

Now that we were preparing to open a new restaurant, it was engendering a great deal of attention. Ironically, the customer anticipation and enthusiasm was greater than that of the suppliers and I was taken aback when our chef Chris Galvin told me, prior to opening, that many of the vendors were convinced we were going to fail, as the ambition and scale of operation was untried, untested and doomed, and that unless we personally guaranteed the supply payment they wouldn't deliver. These moments challenge and the elusive confidence that is essential to opening any successful business was fast receding. I had to back myself, so I told him to tell those suppliers that if they weren't supplying us, without guarantee, by the day we opened then they would never supply us again. Some decided not to until they saw that we seemed to have a success and then were over-solicitous in trying to join the roster. They have never supplied me again.

Against the background of this, soon after opening I found Charles Saatchi sitting by himself at a table in the centre of the room and he beckoned me over. 'Sit down,' he said. 'How is it going? Lots of problems? Customers getting angry because they can't get in, I bet, lots of threats?'

'Well, yes,' I replied, 'but I do understand them getting annoyed as they have been supporters over the years – as they very forcibly point out.'

The words were hardly out of my mouth before Charles was quick to dismiss this people-pleasing notion. 'They are not "supporters" – you owe them nothing. They come to your restaurants because you create wonderful places where they are served very good food really well, at reasonable prices, and where they are treated as special and better than anywhere else.'

This made me uncomfortable (I am British!) but as I protested, he went on: 'Supporters are people who come to you when you are not so busy or in demand, when you make mistakes, are learning and trying your best with mixed results and depend on their support and belief to see you through. By the same token real supporters are happy for you if you turn them away.'

He was right. I had learned something. You have to recognise when you are doing a good job as much as when you are doing a bad one – and be sure to see that just as much. As it happens, within minutes I was confronted by a grande dame at the desk who was causing a big scene, shouting at the staff that it was ridiculous that she couldn't get a table as she had been a great supporter over the years and unless we gave her the table she wanted, she would tell all her friends never to come, and nor would she ever again.

The 'people-pleaser' in me winced, but grasping Charles's words about the difference to my heart, I said to her, 'If this is what you call support then I think I will opt for your enmity.'

I was emancipated and thereby propelled on a path of discovery whereby I learned that candid, straightforward honesty about my feelings garners respect rather than enemies.

# Authority

You become an authority when people trust, believe and respect you. I consider authority to be the biggest quality that any company can aspire to. For restaurants that earn or possess authority there will be a much easier passage through to success.

Let me explain through the medium of chicken soup with matzo dumplings – the *sine qua non* of Jewish cuisine and culture. When we opened The Wolseley we had the temerity to put it on the menu, and we doubled down by adding chopped liver.

As my once-mother-in-law would say, 'Oy vey!'

I was reasonably confident we could get it right, especially being the father of Jewish children, but come the impending opening the recipe had got lost in translation and the dumplings were, to my mind, a bit hard. After much debate we went with them as they were and it was therefore no surprise to me when an early customer, who had grown up on chicken soup, told me that they had enjoyed the experience 'but the dumplings were too firm'.

I could only agree.

And when the next departee said, 'Great place, Jeremy – pity about the chicken soup dumplings.' I nodded: 'Too firm?' 'Not at all, came the answer, too soft!'

We softened the matzo ball dumplings and yet the complaints continued to come in, and as the basis of them widened I started to get rather irritated. Everyone thought they knew better. Often the complaint was accompanied by the statement 'I will give you my mother's/grandmother's recipe – it's the best' (never the wife's, I noticed, and always the man moaning) until when I was offered, very condescendingly, yet another 'best recipe in the world' I rather tersely responded,

'Please do, I would really appreciate that', and waited for the smug smile to appear before adding, 'That will bring my collection of "best chicken soup" recipes up to 500.'

I know, bad of me, but it was twenty years ago and now I wouldn't ever rise to that sort of bait or baiting.

My remark was overheard by a beloved Jewish–American customer at the neighbouring table who beckoned me over, saying, 'I don't think I have ever seen you so tetchy before, what exactly happened?' When I explained, he wagged his finger in disapproval.

'You are playing it all wrong. Here's what you do.' He asked if I knew the name of the English equivalent for the American mashgiach, the man you find in a kosher kitchen who checks that the food is indeed kosher.

'A shomer,' I said.

'That's it. So what you do is when anyone complains that the chicken soup or chopped liver isn't right you just fling your arms wide and say, "I know, I know – but the shomer insists we do it this way" and then get away quickly. They will be left wondering whether you really have a shomer and certainly it will shut them up.'

It worked, but I hardly needed to use this device because not long afterwards I realised that the complaints had dried up. And now we come to the point of this illustration; by then we had been open six months, had established a following and were perceived as a success. People stopped daring to criticise because they would be 'going against the norm'. We had achieved authority.

# A day in the life of The Wolseley

The Wolseley opened its doors to the public in November 2003. It was a 165-seat-capacity restaurant, taking orders from 7 a.m. till midnight, serving breakfast, lunch and dinner. Unlike Le Caprice and The Ivy, it was a success from the very beginning, and for a time was reputed to have the highest-grossing turnover of any restaurant in Britain.

Interestingly, few thought it would work, but in truth it was the sort of restaurant we enjoyed on the continent but only craved here. Many a restaurateur would say to me after it proved successful: 'I thought of doing that', and I would slightly pointedly reply: 'But you didn't.'

Here is an account of a day in the life of The Wolseley witnessed and recounted by Simon Davis for the *Evening Standard* in 2012. I am grateful to Simon Davis and the *Evening Standard* for allowing me to reproduce this.

SIR TERRY WOGAN his spinnaker up, strode into The Wolseley on Piccadilly last Wednesday and positioned himself for all to see in the horseshoe-shaped 'inner sanctum' – the culinary equivalent of sitting in the Royal Box at the opera. And who should join him for lunch? Why, Kevin Lygo, director of Channel 4. BBC veteran Wogan has already vented his annoyance at Jonathan Ross's £18-million wages. Post Michael Grade, are more defections on the cards?

You see, savvy players know that if you want people to sit up and take notice, you don't issue a press release. You tread the boards of The Wolseley. For that is what this all-day brasserie on Piccadilly is, a stage upon which the more succulent scenes of London life are played out, and anyone can get a ticket.

But is it really like that? Have owners Jeremy King and Christopher Corbin (formerly of The Ivy, Le Caprice and J. Sheekey) really created a place where Damien Hirst drops in for porridge, Madonna for tea and Ralph Fiennes sits eating a burger and learning his lines?

I decided to find out. So one day last week I arrived at 7am when the ornate iron doors of the former car showroom, next door to The Ritz, swung open, and didn't leave until 1am the following day. (I moved tables to avoid DVT, as 18 hours is the same as the flight time to Perth.)

By 7:15am the place is filling with thirty-something men in crisp open-necked shirts, blue suits and heavy watches. There must be 60 of them and they sit, in pairs, chatting animatedly.

It is a wicked irony that a restaurant in which one lusts to eavesdrop has vaulted ceilings so cathedral-like that conversation is sucked up into a vortex. (King later explained that acoustic engineers from an opera house advised on the best place for tables.)

I collar a waiter to ask after the spruced-up buccaneers eating fruit salad and eggs Benedict. 'They work in hedge-fund offices in Mayfair,' he tells me. 'The Asian markets open at 6am and they come here after initial trading.'

I order tea, grapefruit juice, Bircher muesli (very in) and kippers. By the time the kippers are served – good too, lightly poached then grilled as they should be – the first women arrive on the scene.

Apparently this twenty-eight-year-old has a shop on Mount Street and hosted a party for her friend, Kate Moss, in Bali this summer. (She had porridge and honey, which is very fashionable apparently, as is the carrot and ginger juice and the boiled egg with soldiers.) It's all reasonable, too. The full English costs £12.50. It's £28 at Claridge's.

'Business, beauty, brains and bull-shitters are all under one roof here,' says Geordie Greig, impish editor of *Tatler*. It is not clear which category he comes under. 'Like the Colosseum, no one has a bad view.'

Sir David Frost is eating bacon and eggs with a friend. I table hop. 'So, do you like Frost/Nixon?' I ask him of Peter Morgan's play, based on his 1977 landmark interview with President Nixon (which took the Editor's Award at this week's *Evening Standard* Theatre Awards). 'It's a good play,' he says, looking spry. 'And they've much right.'

I ask if it's true that Nixon called him the night before the Watergate scandal broke, as the play suggests. 'That may not have happened,' he smiles, 'but I'm perfectly happy for it to be included.' And off he skips, past a table where Damien Hirst has 'dropped in for some porridge'. 'Damien comes for breakfast,' says a waiter. 'And Lucian Freud is often here for dinner.'

By 10am things thin out and I move into a salon at the front of the restaurant for a coffee with restaurant critic Fay Maschler, who I have asked to join me to tell me why, as a restaurant, The Wolseley has had such an effect on London.

'It's both supremely elegant – a case of where details such as linen, glassware, coffee service, cake stands impinge quietly but potently – and accessible,' she says as we eat a rather average fruit salad. You can buy said glassware. 'The stated aim of recreating a Middle European Grand Café is achieved. You spot people who know how to get the best out of restaurants visibly responding to what this unusually egalitarian establishment offers.'

'Egalitarian?' I splutter. Surely not. But according to MD Robert Holland 30 per cent of all trade comes from people like me, walking in off the street. 'We keep back tables on a first-come, first-served basis,' says Holland, who reveals that a staff of 130 waiters, chefs, doormen, baristas, washer-uppers and managers are needed and that the only downtime is between 2am, when the last staff leave, and 3am when the pastry chefs start baking. Oh, and they use four tonnes of coffee a year, and 8,000 eggs a week.

In his light grey three-piece suit, King tilts his towering frame towards Sir Peter Hall, who is having lunch to celebrate the fine notices for *Amy's View*, which he has directed and stars Felicity Kendal. King, who worked at Joe Allen's in the early Eighties (Corbin was at Langan's), has a deference and professional charm that is borderline eerie.

'He's a brilliant restaurateur but I wouldn't want to work for him,' says a Wolseley regular who won't be named because they want to stay a regular. They are taskmasters, I gather, but to make this place run as smoothly as it does – the service is remarkably unflustered and accurate – they need to be.

I have lunch with television executive Zad Rogers, son of architect Sir Richard, who along with his business partner, Kirsty Wark, recently sold their production-company IWC to RDF. I have a Bloody Mary – it's been a long morning – plus snails and confit of duck. It's all excellent and just as good as Brasserie Lipp in Paris or Balthazar in New York, two establishments which are influences.

Dawn French is having lunch with some friends on the eve of her new BBC show *Jam and Jerusalem*. There is a ripe moment when Sir Peter Hall comes to give her a kiss on the way out. His stately frame is unable to stoop while she struggles to raise herself up (it turned out later that she had pulled a muscle). They compromise with a hand stroke.

On the table next to me sit a couple in their fifties who look as if they'd be handy at a village fete. They order a late lunch of Cornish crab, croque monsieur and Champagne. 'It just looked so lovely from outside so we came in,' they tell me. 'We're from Stevenage. Do you know it?' They'd never heard of The Wolseley and why should they? 'We are in town to do some Christmas shopping.'

Between lunch and afternoon tea the place never empties. I had the best cheesecake I have ever eaten but other couples come in for Matjes herrings with beetroot or warm chicken soup, a group of five chit-chatty housewives gossip over finger cakes and in the corner, alone, Ralph Fiennes orders a burger and talks to himself. He is learning lines for Beckett's play *First Love* in which he will star during the Sydney Festival. He likes coming here because he is left alone, he can eat what he wants at any time of day and he feels 'part of London'.

I am into my 13th hour when the place moves into dinner mode. There are lots of families with young children scoffing fries and suckling pig before the theatre.

My guests for dinner are the actor Johnny Standing and his journalist wife Sarah, both regulars. 'It manages to turn any small event into a grand occasion,' says Sarah. There could be few smaller occasions than dinner with me but the place was throbbing.

And so the night goes on. People are still ordering dinner at midnight. At 12.43am, a kindly Mr Holland gives me a glass of 1975 Armagnac to celebrate. 'You've been here longer than any of my staff,' he says.

I certainly couldn't have captured the feeling of that day better myself. It is important to remember, however, that this is effectively a snapshot; a few frames from a movie that plays every day with an ever-changing cast but with the same scenery. Except, of course, the truth is that it is the clientele and staff who really are the scenery as well as the lead actors.

# Friends can sometimes be foes – and still remain beloved

My early encounters singled out Adrian Gill as, well, dare I say it, a bit of a prat. With his tartan plus fours, deer-stalker and monocle, I was happy to avoid him. I should add that most drunks filled me with antipathy. Not all, though – I have always been very fond of writer Peter Ackroyd, who happened to buy the house I was living in at The Angel, Islington. This was Duncan Terrace, which he was proud to have single-handedly managed to rename 'Drunken Terrace'. Although my patience nearly gave out on him after he almost drank himself to death. It was on the occasion of him being rushed to hospital in 1999 and lapsing into a coma due to a heart attack resulting from the pummelling he had given his body over the years. I then found myself in charge of the hospital support obligations as 'family', and on arriving at the hospital asking the matron if I could have a word with him. 'I'm not sure he'll hear you,' she replied, and I suppose she anticipated that I would whisper soft words of love and encouragement as opposed to the 'You fucking idiot – I told you this would happen if you carried on this way – it's all your own fault' that I yelled at him (I used to swear in those days). Peter claimed afterwards that he remembered me shouting at him and rather enjoyed it.

There were others for whom I retained tolerance, love and understanding, with Peter Langan being a good example. Terence Baker being another. Terence was a theatrical and TV agent/producer who perjured himself on behalf of Jeffrey Archer not long before a premature death at fifty-two – the cursed drink being the culprit. I smile, though, at the memory of Terence one night cycling through the front door of a still-full Le Caprice at 12.15 a.m., and was still on his bike when he got to the rear of the restaurant and found me. 'Dinner for one and my bike, Jeremy, my good man!' And having been told it was too late and the kitchen was closed he asked what the time was. On hearing he stared at his watch (my memory is of an old-fashioned Rolex), then took it off shouting, 'Fucking useless watch.' Then having attracted the attention of the restaurant, he proceeded to stamp on it until it smashed and rode off back through the restaurant. They could be fun . . .

But I digress. This chapter is about one particular man who managed to save himself from the drink and, despite being seriously dyslexic, went on to be one of the most spectacular writers of our generation.

He was a great reader, too, and although reading a book took him at least five times longer than most of us, his capacity to absorb and repeat what he had read was a similar coefficient. His capacity to summon up information was remarkable and it was indeed a brave person who contradicted him. Coupled with one of the greatest appetites for experience, information and the unusual, he was a powder keg of knowledge.

I have spent an inordinate amount of time counselling 'working alcoholics' amongst my staff and there was no one better for advice than Adrian who, at the age of thirty, got himself into recovery and became the poster-boy for Alcoholics Anonymous. He was remarkable in how assiduously he embraced the twelve-step recovery and the necessity of attending meetings – it seemed to be the one part of his life where he could resist cynicism and I loved him and thanked him for all he had done for so many people.

We were very different – confidence meeting diffidence, addiction encountering restraint, opinion meeting discretion – and yet fundamentally incredibly similar; and I adored this troublesome quasi twin (we were born one week apart, with him being the younger). So there was an acute but suppressed empathy and admiration for him, and although I wasn't initially so impressed by his persona, there was no denying the brilliance of his writing. And it is remarkable to consider just how quickly his reputation developed from a 1991 debut (well done

*Friends can sometimes be foes – and still remain beloved*

Jane Proctor at *Tatler*) into a prized writer for the *Sunday Times*. Our relationship particularly came alive after the relentless badgering of the literary agent Ed Victor for us to write a book about The Ivy. Neither Chris nor I had the necessary hubris and were resistant to the idea until I ventured we wouldn't be averse to someone else writing a book about the restaurant. Seizing upon this, Ed started suggesting writers (mostly his clients, it has to be said) but the person we wanted was Adrian. Why? His writing was so perceptive about restaurants in particular, and of course his turn of phrase made the page come to life, and I regaled Chris and Ed with some of my favourites.

*'But they also confuse two distinct occupations: cooks and chefs. Cooks do it at home for love. Chefs do it in public for money. Dinner parties are karaoke cheffery.'*

*'Be careful trying to jump on a band wagon. In running to do so you might lose your footing and fall flat on your face.'*

And in one of the most elegant of statements about the old 'White Elephant on the River's' signature dish:

*'Goose or Duck's Liver is an essential part of Tournedos Rossini, but if anyone can prove to me whatever it was I ate had ever seen the insides of a goose or a duck I swear I will suck the maître d'hôtel's comb.'*

That was why I wanted him. Because of his ability to evoke and conjure up far beyond the normal capability of words. You just knew that the maître d'hôtel had greasy, dandruff-infested hair and a shiny suit.

The resultant book was groundbreaking and has since been imitated by many. Adrian chose to write 'A day in the life' of The Ivy and despite my prohibition on naming customers managed to capture the atmosphere, glamour and excitement of a restaurant in its prime. It was helped by excellent design and the first use of black-and-white photos for insights into the back-of-house life.

Adrian went on to write the 'sequel' about Le Caprice, which was less successful as a concept, although with some great writing nonetheless.

When it came to our next book, *Breakfast at The Wolseley*, Adrian was so far behind on deadlines already that he declined, and we were hitched with an eminent figure in the Guild of Food Writers. Sadly, this didn't work out. So I phoned the 'busy' Adrian and found him on a grouse moor.

'Adrian – this Wolseley book – I miss you and need you.'

He agreed to take it on and proceeded to do a wonderful job, to an extent. The extent was such that having read his manuscript I told him that there was no introduction, and the book ended rather abruptly.

'Sorry, darling,' he said. 'The meter ran out.'

He could be exasperating. I ended up writing the introduction and managed to put a few more bob in the meter to achieve a better ending. From his very first line the skills and talent are apparent:

*Breakfast is everything. The beginning, the first thing. It is the mouthful that is the commitment to a new day, a continuing life.*

Oh, that his life could have continued more.

While he was best known for his food criticism, he deserved, and received, greater accolades for his more considered writing that embraced the full gamut of humanity. His care for the indigenous and displaced people of this world was an example to us all.

How we enjoyed his restaurant criticism, though – even when we were the butt of it. Many people wondered whether with such an affiliation he was capable of reviewing neutrally any of the restaurants Chris and I ran. An early positioning on doing his job properly was flippantly described as this:

*A food critic really only needs two things in order to do his job properly: no eating disorders and the gastric morals of a hooker with a mortgage.*

But witness this version of the same assertion when reviewing The Wolseley:

*At this point, I have to give you the safety instructions. I have never reviewed The Ivy or Le Caprice, because I wrote both their books (still available). Consequently, I know Jeremy and Chris well, as well as many of the staff who have moved to The Wolseley. So bear that in mind. But then, they also know me well enough to know that if they do their job badly, it's not a reason for me to do mine badly as well.*

Luckily the review was a rave – and you have to admire the promotion of the old books.

He wasn't quite so keen on Fischer's, a smaller, more intimate space on Marylebone High Street which we created in the style of a traditional Viennese restaurant and opened in 2014. Adrian gave only three stars for what seemed a good if not great review. He was rather taken aback to be lambasted by friends for not being more supportive and had to explain that it wasn't him who awarded the stars but the subeditors. This would explain the five stars given to The Tiroler Hut in Westbourne Grove, where Adrian found the food 'all inedible, unless you were as drunk as everyone else in the room, or on the death watch at an old people's home.'

Of all the restaurants I 'reviewed' with him, The Tiroler Hut was the most enjoyable, though. The Tiroler Hut was not a new restaurant to review, having first opened in 1967, but it was the venue of an unusual evening with Anya Hindmarch and James Seymour, the husband-and-wife team behind Anya Hindmarch handbags. Here is Adrian:

*'I was taken by the bag lady Anya Hindmarch, an arbiter of soignée sophistication and élan. She says this is her favourite restaurant. She also brought Jeremy King, father of a 1,000-year reich of restaurants, including The Wolseley. I've known him a long time, and I've never seen him laugh until the tears roll down his cheeks. Come to think of it, I've never seen him laugh at all, just give the occasional Pinteresque grin. I'm not really making the full* 'Allo 'Allo!*, Carry On nature of the underground hut live for you. It's as close as most of us will get to a Christmas party in Colditz. At the third time of bellowing "Tomorrow Belongs to Me", I felt something snap, and I now have a cultural hernia. Without irony, The Tiroler Hut is crass, loud, repetitive, drunken, uncomfortable, embarrassing, cringingly stereotypical and tasteless on so many, many levels. Go now – take all your friends. It is possibly the worst venue ever for a first date.'*

Adrian could be so obtuse at times and even embarrassing – and yet his ability to make us laugh and also laugh at himself, always endeared.

One of my favourite 'reviewing meals' with him was at Terence Conran's restaurant Lutyens, which was set in the old Reuters building in Fleet Street, designed by the architect Sir Edwin Lutyens in the 1930s. (Great building, great history, great room, but as a restaurant lacking any real heart or soul.) Despite the reservation having been made under an alias, we were spotted immediately, and with our cover blown we soon found that the restaurant manager had clearly decided to drop all duties in favour of serving us – but she didn't have the measure of Adrian. There was a starter of fried pigs' trotters. Characteristically, Adrian's first question was, 'Are they rear or front trotters? It really makes a difference as the rear are so much better.' A totally unreasonable question and the poor manager was forced to ask the chef and came back to confirm that the chef had said they were from the rear trotters.

'No, he didn't!' I said.

Horrified, the manager said again that he had.

'Am I right in thinking that it is David Burke who is in the kitchen today?' She nodded.

David, the head chef, had worked for me and was a fiery, no-nonsense Irishman. 'In which case, what he actually said was "What a fucking stupid question. God knows which, but if he thinks the rear are better then that's what you tell him they are – whatever makes him happy and smug."' The manager blushed, stuttered, and on we went with our perfectly pleasant meal.

At the end we were approached by David Burke, who raised his eyebrows and said to me, 'You were absolutely right, Jeremy.' I still cherish the sound of Adrian's belly laugh.

He was wicked, too – he derived such pleasure in inflicting on me the Review Meal for the first Ivy spin-off – knowing that I couldn't say anything. This was his opening . . .

*'The Ivy in the 1990s was as close as you could get to a perfect restaurant. It didn't have the best food in the world, or even in London; it*

*wasn't the prettiest or the most sumptuous room; it was a long way from having the finest wine list; it didn't offer a view. But it had that thing, that hospitality umami, a flavour you can't quite describe, that exists only in conjunction with all the other stuff, and is the glutamate that makes good restaurants great. After all my years of reviewing, I can walk into a space and tell you if they have it or not: it's a hum, the noise of a successful, happy, up-for-it dining room that is contented, infused, flirtatious, expansive. It's the noise humans make when they're at table, wanting it to be memorable, and The Ivy managed to create that twice a day, every day, for a decade.*

*You could walk through the cleverly designed entrance that was like standing in the wings of a theatre and know there was no better stage in the city. They used to say, everyone goes to The Ivy – meaning, of course, there's hardly anyone who can get a table at The Ivy.'*

He went on to say (in a damning one-star review):

*'The Blonde and I took Jeremy and Lauren King* [in 2014 I had married the luxury brand strategist and developer from New Orleans Lauren Gurvich], *the same Jeremy who once owned The Ivy and now*

*has a number of other restaurants. I'm usually wary about taking restaurateurs or chefs to review competitors' restaurants, but in this case I must say that Jeremy was the soul of diplomacy and discretion, offering not so much as a sigh or a raised eyebrow of criticism.'*

It was difficult – but at least I got a placemat drawing to remember the evening by.

Adrian left us in December 2016, at the age of sixty-two. Whilst I don't think anyone will quite match the sheer bravura of his writing, I am delighted that *The Sunday Times* and Adrian's children keep alive the spirit of it with the annual food writing competition awarded in his name. For several years thereafter the panel of Flora and Ali Gill, Tony Turnbull, food editor of *The Times* magazine, critic Marina O'Loughlin, Jeremy Clarkson and me would meet in the Private Room of The Wolseley to eat Adrian-inspired dishes: his eponymous omelette with lobster, caviar and hollandaise; steak with snails, and so on. One year we shared out worry beads in honour of Adrian, who always carried them, but the prevailing spirit within this celebration was a deep abiding sadness and sense of loss.

*Friends can sometimes be foes – and still remain beloved*

# Instinct and intuition

It took me so long to trust my instinct – let alone my intuition.

One of the worst examples of denying my senses was early on in The Wolseley's life, when I was asked to interview the shortlist favourite for the job of managing director. Everyone involved in the recruitment process was happy and impressed with the candidate, but I had to sign off on the decision. Within a few minutes of sitting with them I was asking myself 'What are you doing here – this just won't work', and yet an hour later I was offering them the job. I convinced myself that what others had felt must be right. He was with us for many years until I had to end it. Not because they did anything wrong – on the contrary, they were excellent, hard-working, skilled, effective and much more – a wonderful person, but just not right for me. It was so wrong of me to put them through it, although they are very successful now, thankfully.

The upshot was that I did start to trust myself and for years there would exist an understanding with my senior staff that if anyone was holding early stage interviews for positions where I would have the final sign-off, then I had to be notified so that I could go into the interview room and spend two minutes with the candidate. Then I would indicate afterwards whether to progress them or not. That could be overridden if the interviewer felt strongly that I hadn't seen the talent, but it would have to go through me. And it started to pay dividends.

Perhaps it was at The Ivy that I first established a reputation among my staff for having a good gut instinct, after a particularly tricky situation.

I had turned the corner to the Still Room and observed a waiter with a guilty demeanour. I soon saw why – he was in the process of stealing bread. On turning, he saw me with a start. I told him that he was suspended subject to a disciplinary hearing. The wonderful and pragmatic General Manager, Mitchell Everard – another sadly deceased far too early – heard what was happening and remonstrated with me, an unusual event in itself.

'Jeremy, you can't sack him over a loaf of bread. You've seen others steal minimal things and not sacked them, why are you doing this?'

'I know,' I said, 'and believe me I am not re-enacting *Les Miserables*; it's not what he stole it was *how* he stole it' – the way he handled the bread and snapped it in half – 'that man is a thief without question.'

It was my intuition leading me.

It was the first time I had experienced dissent from my team and when, despite the tears and protestations that he 'had never stolen anything in his life before, that he hadn't eaten that day and the shops were shut', I insisted he was dismissed and it engendered a great deal of bad feeling and disgruntlement.

Until . . .

About three weeks later the police arrived looking for the waiter and we explained he had gone. The policemen said we were well shot of him: it had come to light that he was fronting a credit card fraud ring and was copying our customers' card numbers, amongst other crimes. Had he been bringing in clothes for sale very cheaply to other members of staff? 'Yes,' Mitch replied, 'from his brother-in-law's shop?' 'Nope – all stolen goods,' we learned.

The apologies I received were sincere and my intuition was seldom doubted again – apart from by myself.

Sadly, theft is prevalent in all branches of hospitality, and it is important to remember one of the most dispiriting aphorisms I have ever encountered is based on empiric truth. I first heard it from the mouth of one of my more cynical and grizzled chefs: 'They are too nice to be honest.'

It was a hard lesson that I learned when I was appointed as a manager at Charco's, despite the opposition of the Searcys' board to me on account of my youthful inexperience. The doubters were beginning to be justified in this belief as my early stocktakes revealed quite a lot of money missing. I did everything I could to find out who was responsible and was fortunate to be helped in my investigation by a couple who were working there, Gina and Marsha, and who were clearly upset by my plight. They quickly identified a culprit who I was just about to dismiss when the husband of another employee phoned me and said: 'Jeremy – open your bleeding eyes, it is the couple who are ripping you off, can't you see?' I couldn't see other than what seemed a genuine concern including tears of anguish the more my job was threatened. Unfortunately, the number of Iago-like characters that I have exposed over the years leads me to the point where the first line of suspicion has to be the least likely perpetrator. Follow the clues, not the sentiment.

One area where my intuition has served me well is in assessing whether someone should be allowed into the restaurant, and when it's time for someone to leave.

At The Wolseley I got it wrong once, though. It was a Sunday lunch and there was a big, boorish young man in a rugby shirt sitting with four middle-aged women and showing off. Clicking fingers at the staff, shouting instructions – particularly when two younger women came in and he was trying to call them over and send them drinks. I stepped in. 'I am sorry, sir, but I need to ask you to moderate your behaviour and if you accost any more customers you will be asked to leave.' Soon after I found him at the young women's table and so led him away to be ejected, much to the chagrin of his older admirers. He was reluctant to come with me and it was getting tense, and the staff were gathering because they were alert to a potential fracas. As I walked over I was preparing for the fight. I knew all the signs and 'tells' that precede violence – that he would turn to confront me and would look down before hitting me (unless they're a professional fighter, men always do). And, sure enough, as we reached the reception, he stopped moving, turned around and looked me in the eye, and then there was the tell-tale lowering of the eyes, and I was already on my toes ready to avoid the inevitable punch. He looked up again and says: 'Moderate your behaviour! That's the most elegant way I have ever been thrown out of a place. Impressive. Goodbye!'

And I learned that even when I am certain I must give the benefit of the doubt.

# Dilemmas

A restaurateur will be faced with any number of dilemmas in their day to day, and instinct and intuition play a large role in navigating those. What is probably my favourite dilemma would have challenged even the most sophisticated intuition. This was the occasion of a group including Nancy Pelosi (then speaker of the US House of Representatives) taking over the salon just inside the entrance to The Wolseley – we hadn't been able to offer the private room as it was already booked. But all was settled and the Secret Service security team had taken up their positions by the room entrance and outside. All seemed fine.

But what I hadn't allowed for was the occupants of the private room, and as they arrived it became clear it was an all-male Middle-Eastern group. I asked the manager in charge of the private room to try to ascertain who they were as there was no hint in the booking, which appeared to have been made by the only Brit in the room. A little bit later they called down and said that it seemed they were Syrian Generals discussing an arms purchase.

So my dilemma was that I had Syrian Army Generals buying arms overlooking the room in which was seated the most powerful woman in America. What should I do?

Luckily the moment was taken out of my hands by the arrival of actor Damian Lewis, who was not long out of the series *Homeland*, where he played a US Marine who had been 'turned traitor' by Al-Qaeda in captivity and become a serious threat to America.

I can only tell you of the joy of watching as Damian sat down in the lobby to wait for his guest, oblivious to the fact that some US Secret Service had suddenly gone rigid with alarm. I watched them look at him, look at each other, reach for their guns and radio before their brains computed what their cognitively trained reactions had done and wry smiles broke out on their faces. Damian was taken to his table and I spoke to the security and acknowledged what had just happened. After that it seemed natural for me to fess up about the private room occupants, but they seemed relaxed and mercifully the evening closed without incident.

# Perception and pre-conception

Shortly after we opened The Wolseley, in through the door came an old Ivy customer I had hardly seen since his move to Hong Kong in the mid-Nineties. As we got talking, he asked me whether he had ever told me the story of his return to The Ivy on a trip back to London after we had sold the majority share in the restaurant to the Belgo Group in 1998.

He hadn't, so he went on:

'I was interested to see how it was holding up since you had gone, so I booked for lunch. I walked through the door, expecting to be recognised, only to be greeted by someone on the desk I had never seen before and who certainly didn't know who I was, before being taken to a table that frankly was bit of a disappointment – no triumphant return for the lamented, lost regular, that's for sure! An old colleague was waiting for me there and I ordered a drink after a bit of an annoying wait (they used to know my "usual" and have it on the table immediately) and, as I surveyed the clientele, I was not really impressed. It was the same room, of course, and everything appeared the same, but the transformation was manifest and the magic had evaporated. I said to my guest – *If Jeremy could see what was happening now, he would be horrified.*

'And then, you said hello.

'Because you hadn't gone, just sold your majority interest, and I learned that you were staying on – as you did for two more years. And as I looked around the room again, I saw a succession of high-profile customers sat at the tables I coveted and the maître d'hôtel greeted me warmly by name, apologising that he hadn't been at the desk to greet me on arrival. As more familiar staff faces said hello I started to feel that warm glow of being back in one of your places, welcome and belonging. And I also realised that I had arrived with a preconception that The Ivy couldn't be the same as before, and this became a self-fulfilling prophecy.'

A salutary lesson, and I am much warier now of my own proclivity to preordain experience, while being more tolerant of others who fall into the same trap.

There is a further branch of perception that I had been fascinated by, which came from my early days at Joe Allen. I would be given letters of complaint wherein there would be a lamentation of perceived disappointments about an experience listed in great detail that, when analysed, showed that the writer had actually had the perfect Joe Allen experience, but just didn't like it. 'I wasn't offered a drink at the bar, I was shown to a table from where you couldn't see the blackboard (the one normally reserved for stars/royalty), the order was taken too quickly and the food arrived too fast', and so on. My mistake was that I had given the royal treatment to someone who wanted to be a commoner.

These misperceptions reached their apotheosis one evening when we had received a telex from New York; it was Joe Allen himself asking us to look after, with utmost deference, an important Broadway producer who was passing through London. (This rather went against his usual forthright view on table allocation, that 'those who count don't care – those who care don't count'.) It was a difficult evening as we were massively oversubscribed, but the one table I was going to have ready was unquestionably the producer's, the best in the house. There wasn't another table to be had, other than the worst one in the house, closest to the door, in the middle of the entrance area by the cloakroom, which was only free because no one would accept it: 'I would rather wait an hour than have that' was a common refrain. It was peak packed, post-theatre time, with customers four-deep at the bar, and into this mayhem walked my star guest of the evening. Remember, this is pre-internet and Google, so finding an image of him was difficult. But I had an idea and his aura of importance and confidence betrayed him, so I was able to greet the producer by name and ask my assistant to seat him: 'Table fifty-six, please' – phew!

I was talking to another aggrieved languisher at the bar when I was jolted by a loud shouting in my ear with the words, 'You fucking little shit!' (Hang on, hardly 'little'!) 'Who the fuck do you think you are – how dare you?'

I told the producer I didn't understand what he meant. This only inflamed the situation.

'Yes, you do, you arrogant fucker. I know that Joe told you to look after me and yet you try and humiliate me with the worst table in the house! I will have you dismissed.'

'But it is the *best* table in the house,' I interjected. 'I promise you.'

'Don't give me that shit – it is the worst and you know it!'

'Then tell me where you want to sit,' I replied. (Remember, we were absolutely full with the only table available being the ignominious Table 0.)

'Don't you dare do this – you are making it worse, fucker – you know exactly where I want to sit and I don't care who you are keeping it for, I am having that table.' And as he pointed to that worst table, still empty as it was impossible to seat, I graciously conceded and watched, fascinated, as he swaggered his way over, his chest swelled with importance. He surveyed the room to see who was impressed by his landing what he thought was the prime seat, while in truth the patiently waiting guests did look at him and thought (in his own lingo), poor fucker.

And I learned an important lesson in perception and that, while in the UK the prestige tables are furthest from the door, in the US it is the opposite.

There are multiple branches of the need for achieving objectivity and this constant dialogue between objectivity, perception, instinct and intuition.

One of my more enjoyable experiences in this sphere was derived from the preparations for the opening of The Wolseley, and my preoccupation with having a relatively small wine list, in the way of Parisian brasseries or Viennese coffee houses – but with a 'twist' in that I wanted every single wine to be a great example of a style, but also good value. We were convening to taste at my house. Now it is well accepted that perception of a wine can increase due to the quality of the glassware, or indeed reputation, but I wanted to take such experiments forward. So I set a conveniently long table with fifteen whites followed by fifteen reds from which I needed approximately ten final choices. The challenge to the panel was that, unlike most tastings which are graded in the ascending order of price and quality, the bottles were shrouded in foil and unidentifiable. There was a simple diktat: 'Tell me how much you would happily pay for each wine.'

The results were fascinating. Some simple wines were rated at twice their normal selling price, much higher than some complacent grand wines with nothing particular to offer other than their pedigree. We had created a wine list that the staff could comfortably attest to in terms of quality and value. If we open our eyes to truth we are no longer obfuscated by perception or reputation or, truth be known, a reliance on past achievements.

# Is it in the stars?

'Surely you don't believe in that astrology bunkum?'

But I do. Let me explain.

I had just arrived back from New York on a day flight and went straight to the office above The Wolseley. On coming down to the restaurant, around 8 p.m., I was confronted by the sight of an ambulance and police in front on Piccadilly, with the duty manager seemingly involved. There had been a knifing outside, but apparently purely coincidentally, so I left the emergency services to it.

On going into the restaurant I could feel a high energy (seasoned restaurateurs can always sense when a room is wrong) and was immediately confronted by a manic customer outraged by the fact that they hadn't been sat in the area they had requested – all spit and splutter – and as I struggled to evade him I noticed that a guest on one of the two front tables was struggling to stand up and then suddenly vomited onto the table.

Hmm . . . So I turned to the maître d'hôtel and asked him to check whether it was a full moon. This was not the first time I had made this request – not by a long way – because over the years I had started to learn that whatever my logical left side of the brain said to the contrary my right side remained adamant that there was something in the notion of astrological determination.

As a schoolboy there was a massive surge in popularity in horoscope reading and it had never gripped me for the simple reason that the newspapers couldn't decide whether my birthday, Midsummer's Day, 21 June, rendered me Gemini or Cancer – by dint of being on the 'cusp'. In later life I was told I needed to have my time of birth to ascertain which was my sign, but asking my mother turned out to be a fool's errand; she had seemingly tried to expunge all memory of that day: 'Longest day of the year, you say? Longest day of my life, that's for sure.'

My father expanded on the day's events. How my mother's first words to me were, 'That's not mine.' Seemingly on account of the fact that I was so battered and bruised. 'I wanted to call you Richard,' said my father, 'but your mother said it was "common" and insisted on Jeremy.' All right, but why on earth 'Bruce' for a middle name? 'Ah yes,' he went on, 'that was your mother's idea as well. You see, she thought you looked like the boxer Bruce Woodcock – known as "the ugliest boxer in the world" – and wanted to name you after him.'

Truth is, she didn't even like the name Jeremy, as I learned early in life. At three years old I saw that the maker of the delicious Sugar Puffs was running a competition to name the Brown Bear mascot they had chosen to promote their new cereal. When I told my mother that I wanted to enter she asked what my name choice was and I, of course, said 'Jeremy'.

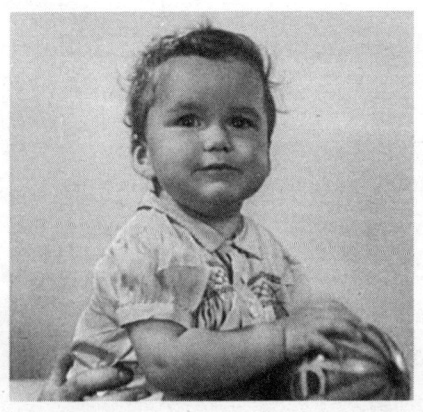

She was tricky, my mother.

'That won't win – Jeremy is a stupid name.' You can imagine my hurt on hearing that. And indeed how the hurt turned into resentment when 'Jeremy' won the competition. (My mother had a lot of impressive characteristics, but mothering was not one of her more natural attributes.)

I still don't know my star sign. But that doesn't detract me from having a reluctant belief that there is some truth in astrology. Certainly, the effect of a full moon is manifest, and when living on the Thames I would always know when it was that time in the lunar calendar because the river would appear to empty. How the emergency services gear up at the same time for more problems on a full moon and how I can always immediately feel it in the restaurants, in my sleep patterns, in the behaviour of pets. This shouldn't surprise anyone – after all, what is the derivation of 'lunatic'?

But it goes far beyond this and in particular I metaphorically 'sat up' when I encountered the notion of the Mercury retrograde. It was particularly at a time when trying to extricate ourselves from a very disappointing relationship with our investor in the early days of The Wolseley. Things kept going wrong with the contracts and I heard the refrain 'Ah, of course – Mercury is in retrograde.' So much so that I decided to speak to an old friend, customer and astrologist, Shelley von Strunckel. She said that four times a year Mercury, which circles the Sun much quicker than the Earth, appears to be going backwards and at this time all communications seem to be affected. Computers and phones act up. People miscommunicate, letters go astray, and in fact anything to do with human interaction seems to go awry. She explained she won't allow friends or clients to undertake any new venture or sign contracts during this period. Life, of course, can't stop, but I would always issue a notice to staff when Mercury was in retrograde because it meant tempers were less frayed, frustrations were more muted, electronic failings less exasperating. And to this day I am wary and respectful.

Shelley also gave me wise counsel when I related that my investors at the time were trying to cheat and extort more money than they deserved and were thoroughly and shamelessly vicious in their pursuit of money. Shelley's advice was so pertinent that I have oft repeated it:

*'Jeremy. Let them take your money – you will always find a way to make more – that is, unless you let them also take your soul. You must keep calm, not let them get to you – guard your soul and you will always be fine.'*

Advice I have had to observe with most of my backers.

# Money

I have spent many years fascinated by the corrosive effect of money. It is astonishing how many a customer feels that money entitles them to do what they want in a restaurant and that anyone can be 'bought'. I have always been more impressed by those who are disdainful of money rather than those obsessed by the need for it.

I particularly remember the unreformed early Russian visitor to Le Caprice in the 1980s who rounded on me after I had told him to stop harassing two ladies at the bar. He was wide-eyed and splenetic and as he reached for his pocket I momentarily wondered whether it was for a gun. No, he pulled out a thick roll of banknotes and thrust them into my face, saying: 'See! Now fuck off,' which of course elicited my response. 'No, it is you who is doing the fucking off. NOW.'

But, of course, some staff are prone to bribery when it comes to finding a table, even though I banned it (despite what you may think, bribery is very common and it creates great tension amongst staff). I always relished telling my teams the story of a maître d'hôtel I worked with at Joe Allen getting his comeuppance.

Joe Allen was a very 'hot table', and through the door came an American man asking for a table. He was told we were full.

'I bet if I gave you a hundred pounds you would find me a table.'

Tim on the desk looked around, tempted, wondering if he could get away with it – £100 in 1979 must be about £500 or more nowadays. He acquiesced and naughtily led the man to a prime table, whereupon he was given £10.

'We agreed a hundred pounds!' he said, aghast.

'We were just establishing that you are a whore – now we are negotiating.'

And there was no way of removing him now.

I've seen for myself the disparity in the importance that people ascribe to money – it's certainly not tied to how much of it you have – and was never sure how to make sense of this. I am grateful to the late Australian comedian and satirist Barry Humphries for the definitive story that I needed to help understand it.

Not long after we opened The Wolseley I found an unexpected Barry Humphries sitting at a corner table, and as I approached he sang out:

'Jeremy! I didn't expect to find you here on a Saturday lunch . . . I thought you would be out spending your millions!'

To which I replied, 'Barry, may I just say, a) I don't have said millions – I still need to work for a living; b) You have more millions than I ever will have, and c) that was a really crass thing to say!'

'I know, I know, please forgive me,' he said. 'The thing is I've been touring Dame Edna [his most famous creation] in America and all that anyone seems able to want to talk about is money. By way of an apology, I'm going to tell you a story that I think you will like.

'Whilst I was doing my run in New York I received a call from Joseph Heller [author of *Catch-22*]. Joseph and I and another friend were very close when we were young and poor and have always stayed close. Our other friend had gone on to make billions as a hedge funder and was suggesting we come out to Long Island to see his new house and have a simple lunch "on the deck". So Joe and I get driven out and as we are approaching the house along an impressive drive we pass the multi-car garage and the guest house and our friend's separate office to find an imposing house set between the sea and the pond. Beautiful.

'Said "deck" is some 150 feet long and lunch is served, but our host is distracted, getting interrupted and not able to relax, resulting in him departing the table early and leaving Joe and I to enjoy the post-prandial drink and view across the water.

'I say to Joe: "Isn't this amazing?" and he agrees.

'I go on, "I bet you would love to have this place?" and "Of course" comes the reply. So I thought I would stir him up and asked, '"Tell me, Joe – be honest – just how envious are you?"

'At this he becomes quite agitated and angry and declares, "Not at all."

'"Oh come on, Joe, you must be – you said yourself how you would want all this."

'"That's true, but I'm not envious of him and don't you dare suggest otherwise." I pressed him further, and he said, "I am neither envious nor jealous and the reason is because I have *more* than him."

'"Joe, don't be silly. *Catch-22* served you well, but how can you say you have more than him – he has billions! There is no ignominy in a bit of envy."

'"I do have more than him: I have enough, and he never will."'

(I've since learned that this same story was immortalised by Kurt Vonnegut in his poem 'Joe Heller', published in the *New Yorker* in 2005.)

And therein lay the truth about so many of the rich. However much wealth they have, they are still capable of resenting that others might be richer, have a bigger yacht, a 'fitter' spouse. I know people who earn £30,000 a year and have enough. They would like more but they can still be happy. And I know people on £30 million a year who have nowhere near enough, and the happiness they thought money would bring proves elusive on many counts.

A coda: I have always admired Joseph Heller and he had always seemed to me what the French call '*bien dans sa peau*' (comfortable in his own skin). The story I most like about him was when he was being interviewed for a feature, I think in the *New Yorker*. The interviewer started off with this:

'Joseph Heller – iconic writer – and who hasn't read *Catch 22* or indeed seen Mike Nichols' film? Truly a great book of our times. But let's face it, you have never written anything as good since, have you?'

Heller paused before answering laconically, 'No, it's true – I haven't. But then again, nor has anyone else.'

*Touché.*

# Luxury

The Merriam-Webster Dictionary would have luxury as *'An indulgence in something that provides pleasure, satisfaction, or ease.'* When asked for my own definition of luxury, I believe that the answer should be 'Time'. In the past, however, I often gave the more glib reply: 'Silk underwear.'

Now, I don't wear silk underwear myself, but I do like the notion that doing so feels really good and is really only for personal indulgence. It's expensive, yes, but it's likely only very few people are aware that you are wearing it. And that is at odds with what, sadly, too many people view luxury as – an extravagant and ostentatious display of wealth.

In 2014, I realised a long-held ambition of opening a hotel, The Beaumont Hotel in Mayfair. Wanting to better understand what people looked for in their choice of hotel, I asked the celebrated architect Lord Norman Foster what made him so dedicated to his own favourite hotel, The Berkeley.

'Because it all just happens,' he said. He elucidated by saying that after initially establishing what he and his wife wanted in terms of their room and service it just always happened – and there was no member of staff pointing out how clever they had been by ensuring it. That's real luxury.

It was in the process of opening The Beaumont that I really began to explore and have fun with the idea of conceiving every new establishment around a unique story. I came up with the story of a fictional Jimmy Beaumont opening the hotel in the 1920s and wrote this down in a document that I shared with the team – this focused the thinking on creating the hotel with a clearly defined look and period consistency.

A month later, I was at a project meeting when we were discussing the new lighting designer, and was asked by the director if it was all right to give him a copy of my 'History'? Note they said history. Now, since distributing it, I was actually ready to embellish the 'Story' and asked that they wait a week because 'some new facts had emerged'. (I was getting into the spirit of things.)

'Oh really, such as?' said the director.

'Well . . .' I hesitated. 'You know how I mentioned that Ernest Hemingway and Scott Fitzgerald used the Beaumont's "Cub Room" Bar before the war? Well . . . I happen to have a first edition of Hemingway's *The Sun Also Rises* (not true then – although it is now) and I chanced to be leafing through it the other day and caught sight of the dedication. Now, you won't believe this, but the book is dedicated to Jimmy Beaumont.'

'Oh wow, amazing, incredible – we must feature this,' was the gist of the responses. I am gobsmacked by their reaction and tell them that I have just made this up – like the rest of the 'history' – and they are palpably disappointed.

It taught me how the power of storytelling is paramount. Continuing this method through the food, décor, uniforms – yet with a modern twist – greatly enhances the experience. The modern twist is crucial, because we mustn't fall into the trap of pastiche, nor trying to create a

museum manqué. It must seem that the hotel of the 1920s, whilst recognisably of the period, has evolved as it would have if actually original.

But back to luxury. In a world that equates luxury with affluence there are other elements that I feel are more accessible and can't necessarily be bought. Love is a prime example – accessible in theory to all but elusive to so many and hard to buy. In restaurant terms, having someone know your name, being happy to see you, wanting to indulge you, irrespective of what you are spending, is precious.

And this where it gets interesting for me, because I would often find it hard to reconcile my feelings of egalitarianism with a world that is invariably privileged by money. At a dinner party with writer, filmmaker and political commentator Tariq Ali thirty years or so ago, a rather aggressive fellow guest started to lay into him, asking how he could possibly justify his love of fine claret and hand-made shoes with his professed socialism? 'Simple,' he replied, 'I devote my life to the belief that *everyone* should be able to enjoy the same.'

While not everyone will be able to afford an expensive claret, it really is possible to luxuriate in the glory of good service without having to buy it. Good manners, courtesy, consideration, empathy and kindness repay the purveyors so that often the rich are envious and jealous of the attention that is earned rather than achieved through a transaction.

Not that long ago I was very struck by the opening of a Mayfair club that had solicited the help of celebrities to attract members. And it seemed to be working. I hadn't been myself, but soon after the launch I collected Lauren from a dinner. As I walked through the room I realised that I recognised most of the hosts as being previous customers of mine and felt a frisson of concern that they were no longer. I stopped to consider this, and then I quickly realised that I had lost many of them over the years because they hadn't been indulged at my restaurants when they tried and failed to buy prime tables and garner preferential attention with banknotes. I took a few more steps and then stopped again, sensing there was something wrong. It was a moment before I understood what: there was no atmosphere. There was no joy, no friendly chatter, no buzz of friendship and conviviality. Yes, there was the perceived luxury of being in a 'soignée' establishment, the luxury of fine Champagne and wines, the luxury of a doorman-tended Bentley, but where was the real luxury of someone truly caring – whether the companions or staff?

# Hospitality

In a March 2023 article in the *Financial Times* titled, 'What is it about British hospitality?', columnist and restaurant critic Tim Hayward ruminates on the nature of hospitality and the expression of it in other countries, bemoaning the fact that there seems to be no English equivalent word or phrase for the Spanish '*Buen provecho!*', Greek '*Kalí óreksi!*', or Swedish '*Smaklig måltid!*'. 'There's nothing,' he writes, 'nothing in our culture that helps us express that we welcome you and hope you're going to have a good time while we look after you. All we can do is nick "*Bon Appetit*" from the bloody French.'

Perhaps historically we have been up against it because we don't have what I call a 'market mentality' to cooking and feeding people, in the way of the French, Italians and Spanish. In the UK, when cooking at home we generally find a recipe we like the look of, make a shopping list, and then try to find the ingredients – often disregarding seasonal availability. Whereas on the continent home cooks are more likely to go to the market first and then decide what to cook. But for me this is what has made it more challenging, inspiring and exciting over the years to counter the myth of the Brits being unable to be great restaurateurs.

I see hospitality as a state of mind, a genuine altruism, kindness, empathy and generosity that transcends the mechanics of serving food and drink and the design of a room.

It is unfortunate how often its practitioners need to be reminded of the tenets of our trade. I am often speechless to discover that, say, a kitchen repairman is on the premises, responding often to critical failure and yet no one has offered them even a coffee.

I am at pains to tell my reception staff just how important a role they play when it comes to creating a sense of hospitality. Early in 2022

I conducted a series of masterclasses with all the front door staff to emphasise just how important the welcome into a restaurant can be.

On a whim, I started by saying to the assembled team that I was planning to replace them all with Artificial Intelligence – robots. Remember this was early 2022, when AI and robots were not used daily nor seen as such a 'threat'. There was sufficient attention now for me to carry on:

'And why wouldn't I? Robots are never late, never have problems at home, are never sick, hungover, beset with personal problems. So when someone comes into the restaurant they can effectively ask, albeit somewhat mechanically, all the questions you do. *Good evening, do you have a reservation, what is your name, etc.?'* (And don't forget soon they will have Iris recognition so that they don't have to even ask . . .) And on learning the name there is no delay in them finding the reservation – as often happens with yourselves because you haven't spent enough time reading through and memorising the manifest. The robot will immediately respond *and* know the status of the table, whether ready, still occupied, being prepared and will explain as appropriate (no frantic looking behind into the room), and when it instructs the person where to go it will be as it prints out the details of the guest (no 'sorry I forgot' or 'I was too busy'). Much more efficient than yourselves – it all makes so much sense and although there is an initial capital outlay the savings on salary will soon come into play. So why wouldn't I take this course of action?'

There was, of course, uncertainty amongst the team as to whether I was really serious or doing another 'Jeremy' – and so I went on:

'I will tell you why I wouldn't, despite the compelling case for it. Because that robot, however efficient, has no empathy. No intuition nor instinct. And crucially it can't love – all things that you are able to do.

'BUT YOU DON'T!'

In the ever-increasing mechanisation and digitalisation of our world it is crucial that we remember the talents we have as humans and our enduring superiority – for now.

When I was opening The Beaumont Hotel, I asked the front office manager for a script for all elements of the 'customer journey'. He was surprised at this and asked the general manager his thoughts and was told, 'Go ahead, he enjoys the detail and you might learn something.'

When I returned the script, I told him it was exemplary, but only for a traditional hotel going through the motions. We were going to tear it up and look at how we could achieve something much more special.

'When someone walks in and goes to reception, why are we asking whether they have a reservation? What percentage of people turn up at a five-star West End hotel without a reservation? And do we need to ask their name, or can we ascertain it through other means – luggage labels, googling, asking travel agents for photos? Because if we welcome them by name the whole experience is enhanced.'

I hate to be asked whether I have had a good journey. If I feel the need to share the information, it's at my own behest not yours. I don't want to be asked whether I have been at the hotel before – you should know that automatically – and offer to be shown around. Nor do I want to fill in a form.

The 'guest journey' I seek is someone who greets me by name and, for instance, says, 'I see you have travelled from San Francisco. You must be tired so rather than show you around let me have you taken to your room now and we can do that later.' And then here comes the first necessary question: 'Can I send you up a tea or coffee?'

I teach my staff that questions are never to be made unless you *need* an answer. Otherwise, make statements and the guest will turn them into questions should they want to. 'I hope you didn't experience problems with the storms.'

This is how I explained to a crestfallen concierge that had received a gruff response to his question: 'Did you enjoy Legoland today?' (The concierge had arranged the visit.) Of course he hadn't. It had rained all day and he was with young children. However, if you had set it up better, allowing for the forecast rain, then you could have said:

'Welcome back, Mr Smith. I hope the rain didn't ruin the day . . . how about we send up some hot chocolate?' To which he more likely would respond: 'Actually, thanks to you arranging those cagoules it really wasn't bad at all – and we would love hot chocolate.'

It doesn't take much to transform rudimentary service into truly great service.

And here's one final story that I reach for often when I'm asked about what hospitality means.

I received a letter from a customer I hardly knew. He wanted to tell me that he had been at The Wolseley with a new girlfriend; on the way out, they were standing near the reception awaiting their coats, when she looked into the 'salon' and saw the cake display.

'Oh no,' she exclaimed sadly, 'they have Battenberg cake. It's my favourite, I wish I'd known.'

'Next time,' the boyfriend promised.

But, as they settled into their cab a waiter opened the door and handed them a presentation box, saying 'Why wait?', then disappeared.

Inside there were two slices of Battenberg.

However there is an important lesson to further learn from in this ever-stiffening and controlling battle between corporate control and true hospitality. In truth, that inspired waiter should be disciplined for giving away company property without permission and yet if he had followed 'procedure' and found a manager he would have missed the opportunity. So we must empower our staff and when they report the action not be upset when the generosity is misguided.

# Lucian Freud

There are several people who have had a profound effect on our restaurants by dint of their regular presence. Antonia Fraser and Harold Pinter would always bring gravitas, Diana, Princess of Wales, glamour, Leslie Waddington, art authority, and many more either brought fame or infamy – both attractive to any restaurateur. There was one regular who, particularly when at The Wolseley, always added layers of all the above and more – Lucian Freud.

Truth is, in the early days at Le Caprice, Lucian Freud also brought fear; it became a regular prerequisite of his attendance that when he booked, often at the last minute, the staff would have to speak to all the customers and ask whether they had their cars parked outside and if so would they mind if we were to move them. Reason being that if Lucian was driving to dinner it was often a rather haphazard journey and arrival would require parking. I would endeavour to intercept him

and offer to do it because otherwise it could be damaging – his Bentley being a rather good dodgem car.

But it was worth it, of course, and we enjoyed his appearances at Le Caprice and The Ivy together with a disparate cast of guests and companions. We were grateful to him for introductions to Francis Bacon, who particularly liked The Ivy, and we were discussing the possibility of a painting to join the collection there when he died suddenly in 1992. Less welcome, by example, was the writer and photographer Bruce Bernard, who whilst an important player in art history was a significant pain for restaurateurs and was better off at The French House (York Minster, as formerly known), or even the notorious Coach & Horses – all home to the dissolute and louche.

The relationship with Lucian really developed, though, with the opening of The Wolseley, which seemed to appeal to him perfectly because of its Grand Café persona, a hint of Bohemia, flexible hours and a roll call of fascinating customers. He had also given up driving, which was a relief. He seemed at home. The art critic Martin Gayford wrote a little about Lucian's relationship with The Wolseley in his account of sitting for him, in the excellent *Man with a Blue Scarf*:

*'After the sitting is over, about nine o'clock, LF announces: "I'll just change and then we will go out to dinner." Then we take a taxi to The Wolseley, a restaurant that has recently opened on Piccadilly. It turns out to be a huge, animated room, decorated in a sort of Art Deco classical style, in a wonderful building that was originally a car showroom between the wars. It is full of waiters and waitresses dashing about with orders, and a hubbub of conversation at different tables, just like the nicest sort of Parisian brasserie. LF knows one of the owners, Jeremy King, whom he introduces, then tells me King is an expert at judo, a black belt I think, and relates various exploits of his.'*

I should point out that the judo part isn't true, but Lucian and I shared a penchant for imagining the alternative lives of people.

During the last ten years of his life Lucian ate dinner most nights of the week at The Wolseley. He was intensely private and I've never known a person be so clear as to how they wanted to live their life. People would often describe him as 'selfish', which I always thought to be a pejorative word, but I learned through him the inherent honesty of its meaning. It epitomised his approach to life, in that he never did anything unless he wanted to.

One night we had somebody patiently waiting in the restaurant for Lucian and he hadn't arrived, which was very unlike him. Concerned, I called him and was relieved to hear his voice as he reproached himself for not having the date in the diary. I told him that I had assumed he didn't want to come, but he was incredulous at the notion. 'Don't you see?' he said, 'if I didn't want to have the dinner with them, I never would have arranged it.' Obligation was not something that Lucian understood.

It was a lesson that was really important for me – the difference between 'Good Selfish' and 'Bad Selfish' and the importance of looking after our own happiness by stating our needs and wants. Bad Selfish is when you promise one thing and then do the opposite to suit your needs. I had spent my life believing that if I made everyone around me happy then I would be too. This inevitably failed, until I understood that the people in our orbit are much more likely to be happy if we are too.

Lucian has been described as aloof – nothing could be further from the truth. We often had to protect him from the attentions of regular customers who had misinterpreted his friendly wave as an invitation to join him. He fulfilled that Peter Langan paradigm of being as much at ease with a duchess as a taxi driver. As my relationship with Lucian developed, he began inviting me to join him for dinner, if he was alone, or to sample one of the clarets from his cellar, which I encouraged him to bring in. In the thirty-five years that I have been working in this business, he is the only customer that I have ever sat or drunk with in one of my restaurants. I realised at an early age the dangers of drinking when working and consequently vowed never to do so – which had the added benefit of saving me the invidious choice as to whose proffered drink I accepted or not.

Lucian would also invite me to join him if he was dining with someone and the encounter wasn't going well, and he needed a 'jester' or 'mediator'. Sometimes I could help, but other times not so much. I was once failing to invigorate a dinner between Lucian and a venerable actress of a similar age that he had encountered a few times at The Wolseley. It was awkward, and out of frustration I said, 'The problem with you two is that you can't remember whether you slept with each other or not.' Mixed reaction: thunder from the actress and a laugh from Lucian, saying, 'I think you are right.' Before they both convulsed with laughter.

And then the relationship went up to a different level that's best explained by this extract from my diary at the time.

*4 January 2006*

*I am standing in the bar at The Wolseley talking to a customer. He's telling me the story of his ninety-two-year-old guest falling over at Oxford Station on Christmas Eve, breaking his hip and shoulder, and then the saga that ensued . . . at which point I am told by Michael, the maître d'hôtel, that I have a phone call. Is this a 'rescue message' I wonder, and as I am about to tell him 'thanks, but I am fine' he says: 'It's Lucian Freud.'*

*And I know what he wants before Lucian even says: 'Jeremy. I can't get you out of my mind – can we meet for a coffee tomorrow?'*

*'Of course.'*

*And what I already know is that he wants to paint my portrait.*

*How?*

*It was the previous week, on New Year's Eve, when I had been returning from the Turkish Baths at the RAC, that I walked past Christie's Auction House on King Street. A reproduction in the window of Freud's* Man in a String Chair *(1988–1989) caught my eye – it was in the next sale at an estimated £3–4million. As I walked up St James's, I thought about what it must be like to sit for Lucian. Who was the unidentified man and why had he been chosen (it turned out he was the bookmaker Victor Chandler) and suddenly a premonition stopped me in my tracks – Lucian wants to paint my portrait, and I think he will ask. That might have seemed fanciful or wishful thinking but it also felt certain.*

*And he did ask.*

*The next day I arrived at the appointed 9.30 a.m. at Clarke's, in Kensington, where Lucian had breakfast most days, to find an empty restaurant. I wasn't sure if he had forgotten me or whether I was too late to join him for his morning ritual. And then he suddenly appeared, saying once again that I was on his mind. He told me that when he had mentioned it to Susanna Chancellor she had said, 'Well, of course he is, because you want to paint him!'*

*I learned that sittings would be twice a week for a month or so, and then maybe once a week: the portrait head and shoulders. He had no idea how long it would take. 'Would you like to come in daylight or electric light?' I elected for 8 a.m. and the contract was made . . .*

*I dared to tell him of my premonition the week before and he responds, 'I am not normally a spiritual person but something was going on between us.'*

*And now we were walking towards his house nearby and were discussing privacy and his preference for discretion, though he was not bothered if I told anyone that he is 'working from me'. But I felt it best to keep it to myself. We entered into a hallway replete with Auerbachs and passed more as we ascended to the studio room that I felt I already knew so well from photos and paintings. The muted colours, the props and the atmosphere of so many pre-viously admired paintings leapt out at me – it was almost a sensual experience. On the easel was the nearly completed portrait of David Dawson, Lucian's assistant and amanuensis, with his dog:* Eli and David *(2005–2006). I am not sure if I entirely liked it as yet but my sense of anticipation was acute.*

*'We'll start in three weeks if that's ok?'*

*Breakfast at Clarke's*

Of course.

After Lucian passed away in 2011 I realised that, other than my part-ner Lauren, I had spent more time with him than anyone else, whether in the restaurant or the studio. I think eating at The Wolseley used to remind him of Paris in the 50s. When I went with him, David Dawson and Sally Clarke to Brasserie Lipp – just a year before he died, when he opened a show in the Pompidou – he asked us if we thought any of the same waiters would still be working there. It was well over fifty years since he had eaten at Lipp regularly and I think, in that moment, he realised quite how much time had passed and how much of a life he had lived.

That weekend at the Pompidou was an adventure in so many ways. Particularly as an odyssey into Lucian's time in Paris with both his first wife, the artist Kitty Garman and the writer and socialite Lady Caroline Blackwood, with whom he had an affair and later married. The lunch at Lipp was also attended by New York gallery owner Bill Acquavella, who represented Lucian, and his wife, Donna. At David's behest I told Bill the story of Frances Bowes and her ownership of the portrait of me. How it had been rapidly finished when David had called me and asked for a 'final sitting' on the Easter weekend and how I had asked 'Is it really important because remember, I have had five "final sittings" already?' David had said it was at your (Bill's) request and after the Monday sitting it was framed on Tuesday, shipped on Wednesday and sold at Basel Art Fair on the Thursday. On Friday I was aware at lunchtime in the restaurant that there was a table taking an inordinate interest in me, and when I eventually approached it there was Frances Bowes, who looked up, pointed a finger at me, and said: 'I just bought you.' The recently widowed Frances, who lived in San Francisco, was a great collector of contemporary art.

From thereon there was a sequence of consequences. David and Lucian coming into The Wolseley and David complaining that Frances wouldn't lend my portrait to the big Copenhagen show – 'Probably can't bear to part from me, and I wouldn't be surprised if she has it hanging in her boudoir,' I jokingly suggested – Lucian concurring. It was then at a lunch with Tate Modern Director Vicente Todolí that he told me 'I just saw you in San Francisco.' I disabused him of that notion as I hadn't been near there since my marriage, and he said, 'No – we were on an art tour of Frances Bowes's house and there you were – Lucian's portrait of you!'

'Out of interest . . . where was it hanging?' I asked.

'That's the funny thing, it was in her bedroom area.'

Hmm . . . and then I told Bill how she would play games, such as when I met her at a Freud/Murdoch party with her daughter and she introduced me, saying: 'This is Jeremy King. Every morning I wake and look at him,' before reassuring her visibly shocked daughter she was talking about the painting.

Bill laughed and smiled indulgently as I went on, until he put a hand on my arm and said: 'Hey, Jeremy, I don't want to ruin the story or burst your bubble, but I should tell you that she has just asked me to sell you for something bigger.' That shut me up. But then he went on and made me an offer I couldn't refuse. 'When do you return to London?' he asked.

Monday evening, I replied. 'What are you doing during the day?' Nothing particular. 'Then we are taking the plane down to Madrid for the day. The Prado is opening up especially for Lucian as he is choosing from the Goya and Velázquez collections paintings for his joint exhibition. Would you like to come?'

'No, thanks . . . Only kidding. YES!'

And what a day we had. Whether it was gathering around Velázquez's *Las Meninas* or lunch at the exquisite La Trainera fish restaurant where I ate *percebes* for the first time – I can smell and taste them now.

In 2008 Lucian would ask me to sit for him again – this time for an etching plate of me for an exhibition at the National Portrait Gallery. The painting had taken over two years to complete, but sitting for the etching went on for nearly three. Perhaps it is fitting that I close on Lucian with an extract from my diary from that time.

*8 June 2011*

*Will it finish? Will anything be ready in time for the fast-approaching NPG show? Individual sittings are not chronicled because I have lost the book – but my diary records sixty-two sittings between 10 March 2010 and 8 June 2011. On 8 June we actually work quite a lot and David announces before we start that he is going to 'pull' the plate and print whatever happens because it is fully formed enough. As ever I am watching carefully as he deliberates between the etching tool and chalk, and after a long hesitation and self-discussion he picks the chalk. I see him start to 'draw' a line across the plate – lifting to miss the body and then resume. It turns out that he has introduced the background – looks like the fireplace. When Lucian disappears and David appears his first words are 'Oh fuck!' He goes on to say that we can't pull nor print as Lucian has changed the nature of the image and as it isn't etched we would not be faithful to his intent.*

*'Maybe it will just go to the Tate,' he goes on. I am not too worried, as for me the important aspect of sitting was the relationship, not the result.*

*Lucian still talks of how he eagerly anticipates the etching being pulled.*

*15 June*

*Lucian is still in bed – not well.*

*The cancer is taking hold and his painkilling patch is affecting him badly. We sit together on his bed and I tell him tales of lap-dancing at Ben Elliot's stag do – my first and last stag do – he likes this a lot and when Rose joins us he says: 'You must listen.'*

*I give him a letter I had received from the daughter of a family he stayed with in the Scilly Isles after the war and he repeatedly reads it for 30 minutes. Something makes me take this photo.*

*17 June*
*He is confused but we sit and talk and reminisce.*

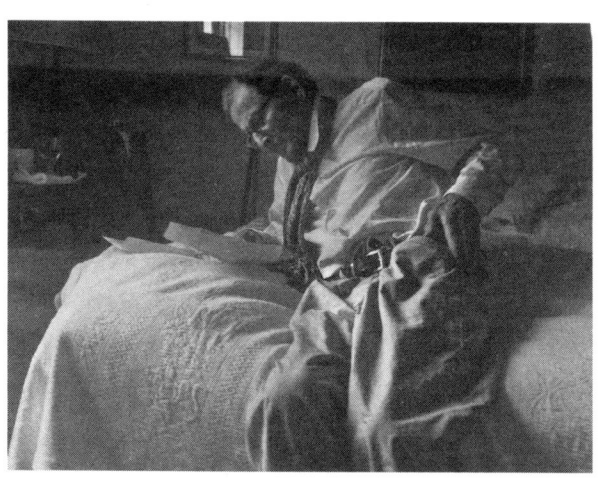

*6 July*
*8 June was indeed the last sitting and today I am visiting in between Jane Willoughby and the Duke of Beaufort. The Duke isn't even properly acknowledged, as Lucian is not leaving his bedroom and is very confused. He bathes and then rests and doesn't get out of his bathrobe. The Duke is immaculate, sweet-smelling and sad – dignified but clearly distraught.*
*The end looks nigh.*

*8 July*
*I realise I might be saying goodbye as I leave for India in the morning.*
*Before I leave, I stop, turn, and say:*
*'Lucian. You do realise that we love you very much.' (I was scared to say 'I')*

'Oh I say – don't go overboard,' he replies.

'I knew that would make you uncomfortable, but nevertheless it is true and I will say it again – I love you very much,' I tell him.

Silence . . .

'Thank you.'

I wonder whether these will be the last words we share.


<u>18 July</u>

I am due to visit Lucian on my return on 19th, but checking in with David he suggests I come Monday 18th. He texts:

'You need to come tonight. Can you get here for 8pm?'

Of course.

I arrive and Lucian has slipped into a deep sleep. Susie [Susanna Chancellor] reluctantly leaves me with him and I watch and listen as he slowly breathes. The wax mask of death is upon him and he looks like a saint from some Spanish sixteenth-century biblical painting. When he stops breathing I am shocked, until after what seems like an eternity he resumes. Then it happens again and I am sure he has gone and call Susie – only for breathing to resume.

I say a few words to him knowing that I won't return however long he lasts, for from here on it would be an intrusion. I don't need the personal validation or kudos. I leave with a hug for David and he suggests I visit Sally, who is dining at Clarke's with the Saumarez Smiths and John Morton Morris.


<u>21 July 2011</u>

I receive a text from David.

'Lucian peacefully left us last night. Diana (from solicitors Harbottle & Lewis) will issue a statement to the Press this evening.

How to react?

I still go to the theatre (Two Guvnors) with Lauren and Hannah. I tell the staff and Dan asks what to do, and after discussion we clear Lucian's table and lay it with a black tablecloth until the end of Friday.

*Geordie Greig, Polly Samson, Antonia Fraser, Ian and Sophie Holm all see and within twenty-four hours it is 'world viral'.*

*Antonia writes subsequently and asks if she can be similarly honoured with a red tablecloth (and a bucket of ice – in case she is going somewhere hot!). I am alternatively numb and sad throughout Friday and decide to eat alone next to his table that night.*

*I miss him so much.*

## The Etching

*David shows it to me again and confirms that it will never be printed because the intention of Lucian must be respected.*

The etching plate now lives in my house – unique in that no print was ever pulled from it – and Lucian lives in my heart.

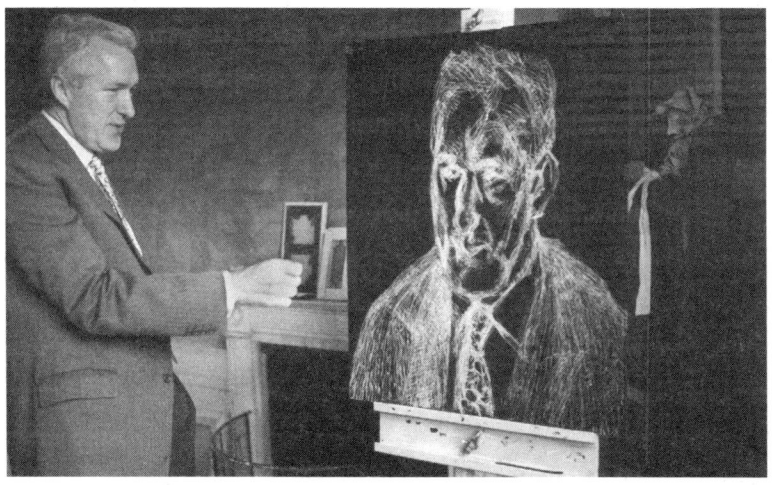

# Part 4: 2020s, a new start

# Change

In 2022, two decades after Chris and I had sold Caprice Holdings and started over, I was once again facing a situation that asked me to pivot and adapt.

In the wake of the Covid pandemic, I found myself in a massive dispute with Minor International, the investors of the Corbin & King restaurants, with the future of the company at stake. The investors had already tried a manoeuvre to put C&K into administration in order to wrest control from us – an attempt that we were able to thwart – and the whole situation was playing out very publicly in the press. Now, we were about to enter an auction to determine who controlled the restaurants.

I found a New York-based fund who were willing to finance the full acquisition. The auction date was set for 31 March 2022. I was concerned we would be outbid, but I was also determined that, no matter the outcome, I would find a way to make it into a positive.

On the day of the auction, a series of legal arguments and delays meant that by 7 p.m. it had still not begun. And at 7 p.m. we were due at The Delaunay with many key figures from the company for a farewell dinner for Helen Smith, who had been Executive Assistant and company secretary for Chris and myself for many years, and who was now retiring. I had thought that we would be announcing the outcome of the auction and fate of the restaurants that evening, but it wasn't to be.

At The Delaunay, the disjointed dinner broke up and I lingered awhile in the dining room. The opera singer Bryn Terfel was there with several other guests, among them Royal Opera House chairman Simon Robey and conductor Mark Elder. They had come straight from the Opera House and were celebrating the closing night of their much-lauded production of Benjamin Britten's *Peter Grimes*. Bryn knew this was a favourite opera of mine, and told his guests as much when I went by the table to greet them. As I stood there, I felt a wave of emotion sweep over me, and I hardly heard Mark Elder asking me why I loved it so much. But I began to talk about the power of the motifs, the sea interlude, and he said that I clearly knew it well. I replied that I could probably sing or hum all the main musical themes.

'Go on then,' he said.

And as Bryn tried to protect me from the challenge, something about the emotion of the evening possessed me and, to their surprise, and indeed also the dozen or so remaining tables of customers, I sang full-voiced the opening line:

'Peter Grimes – Peter Grimes.'

The room went silent, only punctuated by Mark Elder saying: 'That was actually pitch perfect.'

Somehow, I knew it was the last moment I would 'perform' in the restaurants – it was my swansong.

I left the restaurant quickly and walked home to Fitzrovia. I sat down in my office at 12.30 a.m. and the auction finally started at 1.30. As we passed our limit my phone was beeping and ringing from my new investors who were at the administrating solicitor's offices. They went well above, but the counter bids were coming in quickly and it was clear that the soon-to-be-ex partners were determined to win. 'We have to let it go – it's too expensive,' were surprisingly my own words rather than those of the investors, and when they expressed surprise that I was prepared to let go of what I had built I surprised myself by saying somewhat bluntly:

'If you pay any more it will be far too much and I will spend the rest of my working life just paying you off – and I won't have the controls that I had over current investors Minor. We have to let it go.'

And then it was over.

It was 2.30 a.m. and I was looking at a screen. Fortunately, I had already prepared a message to send to the staff, as well as one for my email list of followers, supporters and the press.

I had actually prepared two messages – one of success and one of failure. So I re-read the 'success' one before I sent the 'failure' one. It was probably 3 a.m. so I thought I should try to sleep because I wanted to get to The Wolseley by 8 a.m., but what I hadn't allowed for was that America was still awake and the East was already up. And so the replies started to come in thick and fast – faster than I could keep up with.

It was 4 a.m., and I was typing as quick as I could because I had a feeling I might not get a chance later, and the generous outpouring of concern and condolences demanded a response. I got to bed around 5 a.m. and was up at 6.30 a.m., and as I rushed for the shower I saw that the inbox was filling again rapidly – emails that I would never even see.

Arriving at The Wolseley I found two fellow early arrivals in the office whose tears I attempted to console, but when I walked into the fully occupied kitchen there was a surprising joviality.

'Saw your email, Jeremy,' said the chef. 'We were worried at first and then realised the date – great April Fool!'

I explained the actual situation to a silent audience and then went on into the restaurant where journalists are already assembling and asking questions.

Almost immediately, I was told that the Minor International retinue had arrived upstairs in the office.

There I was stripped of my phone, my laptop, my email accounts – everything – and unceremoniously but effectively thrown out onto the streets.

And it was hard – very hard. But when everyone around you is upset you have a duty to stay strong, stay positive and reject the notion that you can be broken.

Adversity can always be transformed into opportunity.

# Life's transitions

I have watched at close hand the ageing and transitional process that faces us all and been intrigued by the way people deal with it, both physically and mentally. As we age, we have much to reconcile ourselves to; whether we have achieved our potential, behaved with integrity, fulfilled our ambitions, and much more. It is a very fortunate, or an exceedingly delusional, narcissistic, person who is completely at peace with their life's achievements. Ultimately how we morph into old age is largely determined by the mind, and I realise that negativity is fundamentally the adversary of longevity, and positivity is needed both to embrace the success of others and avoid the toxicity that the competitiveness of envy and jealousy can bring. Restaurants are a hotbed of insecurity both among the guests and the restaurateurs themselves, and such traits and the begrudging of success preoccupies inordinately when ultimately the celebration of each other can enhance our own life. Ever since I first heard someone described by a Frenchman as 'Bien dans sa peau' (comfortable in his own skin), I have nurtured the aspiration to be described as thus. However, I do also advocate that true happiness comes through altruism, which is a trait I now feel is crucial to my credo.

Gore Vidal famously said 'Every time a friend succeeds, I die a little', and of course it amuses but ultimately saddens. Although I can understand the sentiment (especially if I underperform against others in the *NY Times* daily Wordle!), I will hopefully remain in the camp of 'Envy is like drinking poison and waiting for the other person to die.'

I have witnessed too much resentment and envy in the crucible of restaurants and have only too often heard the comments that follow in the wake of someone leaving a table early, oblivious to the feelings they have engendered, but the most shocking and incomprehensible manifestation is when it is parental. I take such pleasure in the success of my children and consider their triumphs the joy of life's transition and not a source of jealousy. I still enjoy the memory of standing up to make a speech at a dinner at Jeff Klein's Sunset Tower in LA, where I was promoting the newly opened Beaumont Hotel to the film industry. With his hotel, San Vincente Bungalows Club, and marriage to John Goldwyn, Jeff is a lynchpin of hospitality in Hollywood, and he had kindly wrangled an impressive roster of leading directors, agents and producers, who I was about to address:

'I realise as I look around that more of you actually know my son Jonah than me [Jonah had already garnered success and reputation as a film and TV actor], and I am at that coveted life-transition moment when he is no longer Jeremy King's son and I am now Jonah Hauer-King's father!'

Such great pride for me and subsequently I have experienced the same with both Hannah and Margot and am incredulous that some parents feel threatened by this phenomenon – maybe it is the encroachment of the fear of mortality?

I remember distinctly the moment I made my transition into middle age. It was early in 2006 at The Wolseley. Through the door comes Jools Holland and Dave Gilmour straight from a TV recording of the delicious new song 'On an Island', but they are followed by two grey-haired men who I suddenly realise are Dave Crosby and Graham Nash of Crosby, Stills, Nash & Young – heroes. I say to Matthew, the maître d'hôtel:

'Do you realise who they are?'

And as I tell him, his blank look betrays he hasn't a clue what I am talking about: 'Surely you must know them?' (Although in fairness this was before CSN&Y became known again after Glastonbury 2009.)

'Nope – no clue what you are talking about . . . but here's Katie who knows everything about music – she will know. Katie – Jeremy is excited about the guys who have joined Jools Holland on table one.

They are called . . .' He turns to me and asks once more and repeats: 'Dave Crosby and Graham Nash of . . .' He's forgotten again. 'Crosby, Stills, Nash,' I begrudgingly repeat through pursed lips. Katie is a DJ and music maven who racks her brain before exclaiming, 'Oh yes, hang on, I think my mother had one of their LPs!'

I am now officially old.

And one of the interesting by-products of ageing is that inevitably our children transition into being our parents – assuming they love us. I had the privilege to witness the beginning of this process on 1 April 2022, the day just described, when I lost the battle for control of my company.

Having had my phone taken, I headed to Apple to acquire a new one. I had managed to grab my iPad, which to my surprise started ringing, thanks to Jonah calling – I had no idea it was connected. And this is where he took control. He had been trying to reach me, and, having failed to get through, went to the office where he had the prescience to start taking valuable personal items, until he was stopped by the new legal counsel who accosted him, asking who he was and what was he doing. Jonah told them and countered by questioning them on what they had done to me. The staff later told me he was magnificent. Issuing instructions, he came to 'rescue' me, and soon we were in Vodafone getting set up with a new account and him transferring necessary numbers. He walked me home to Fitzrovia and rustled up his sisters and 'co-parents' Hannah and Margot, who looked after me and made sure I was ok. I will always remember and be grateful for their care and attention and for the joy of the lunch we shared the next day when I don't think I had ever felt more loved. This was set against the background of it also being the day that their mother, Debra, was re-marrying, and yet somehow they lavished their love on both of us and walked this narrow path between the needs of their parents with such aplomb. It readily reminded me of the joy of ageing and transitioning into mutual responsibility and parenthood of those you love most, and at times the necessity of surrendering to the care of others.

*Wedding Day rehearsal 2012 – Hannah, Margot, Jonah*

*The bride to be*

# Embracing change

Giuseppe Tomasi di Lampedusa's *The Leopard*, unpublished in his lifetime, taught me the aphorism, *'If things are to remain the same then everything has to change.'*

Change is a fundamental strength of restaurateuring, while aversion to change is its greatest weakness. The reason it can masquerade as both strength and weakness is that there is a complicity with the customers as the dilemma is acted out with them. If a restaurateur doesn't change a menu there can be approval as well as opprobrium – 'I don't mind you changing the menu as long as you keep my favourite dish on.' It's why there is often the 'main' menu and then an almost equally lengthy list of 'specials', which quickly become a fixture themselves.

A game I play often is occasioned by the winning of an award. I call the management together to congratulate them and then ask the question, 'And how are we going to win this award again next year?' Those who know me well keep quiet and eventually someone comparatively new will fall into the trap I have set by suggesting: 'By maintaining our standards,' to which I tell them that this is the route to bankruptcy.

'We never manage to maintain those standards, they slip imperceptibly and this gains momentum, and whilst our advantage over the competition is eroded by ourselves, they are striving to be better and it won't be long before we are eclipsed. The only way is to constantly improve and, if necessary, completely start again in order to maintain our position. Unquestionably what worked ten years ago has to be reviewed for the present.'

As James Clear, author of *Atomic Habits*, perceptively writes: 'The strategies that made you successful in the past will, at some point, reach their limit. Don't let your previous choices set your future ceiling. The willingness to try new ideas allows you to keep advancing.'

I've seen this play out time and again, in many different ways, during my years in hospitality. The moment you feel yourself slipping into overconfidence, complacency and self-satisfaction, it is time to examine what you are doing – unless you want a rude shock.

Inevitably, this means some hard self-examination and reassessment. Just as a golfer might rebuild their swing, a restaurateur has to, or should, overhaul their systems. As hospitality is one of the most inherently conservative and reactionary bodies, this is not always easy.

I recall a meeting that I chaired in 2010 with eight of my top managers and chefs to discuss a tech innovation that required considerable investment. After a discussion and debate I asked them individually whether they felt we should make the leap and change the operating systems with all its attendant cost.

Each of them said no.

I let them know that I appreciated their thoughts but I had decided we would go ahead with the change.

The quizzical expressions found a spokesperson who asked the question: 'Why would you decide to proceed when we all think you're wrong?'

'Well, firstly, this is not a democracy, it's a benign dictatorship, and secondly, I have had too many of these meetings over the years to believe in consensus.'

I explained that if I had listened to similar groups of managers, chefs or their peers over the years, going back to the 80s, we would not have had computers, email, EPOS (electronic point of sale), electronic reservation systems, paperless credit-card transactions and much, much more. Indeed, I have seen some horrific resistance to innovation that would make working lives so much easier all because of the fear of change. A constant refrain would be, 'Why can't we stay as normal?' which frustrated me so much I eventually put up a sign in the office above The Ivy:

CHANGE IS NORMAL!

I'm often invited to talk to other industries about how they exercise customer care. I am fascinated by how lessons from hospitality can apply to the advertising, publishing, marketing or legal professions. I did once make the mistake of doing a talk to what I thought was IHG (InterContinental Hotels Group) about hospitality and food and beverages in airlines and making it basically a diatribe against British Airways and all their problems at that time – only to discover that I was talking to IAG (International Airlines Group), the owner of BA. Despite their discomfort, they gave the consultancy to the WPP company, Brand Union, that I was meant to be helping. The truth might hurt, but it might also help if told with good intent. This puts me in mind of a William Blake quote taught me by Freud:

'A truth that's told with bad intent beats all the lies you can invent.'

In 2024, my theories about change were put to the test when I once again took ownership of the site of Le Caprice and reopened it under the name 'Arlington'. For many of the old customers it would always be

Le Caprice – they even adopted #notlecaprice even though I wasn't able to keep the name.

The dilemma for me was just how much it should resemble Le Caprice, other than in its appearances. My refurbishment seemingly ended up working a treat: 'You haven't changed a thing!' was the first response (my bank manager would beg to disagree), but I was worried that I might be criticised if I relied on the old menu too much, and yet disappoint if I didn't include Fishcakes, Crispy Duck Salad, Bang Bang Chicken and others. The solution was to ask, so I wrote to all my customer contacts and asked what Le Caprice meant to them. That soon established what people were looking for, with entreaties coming in not just for the classics but even more obscure dishes. The opening chef had worked previously at Le Caprice and was keen to put smoked salmon on because it was a 'good seller', but I explained that was not enough – just as statistics can't determine whether a dish stays or goes. I have seen time and time again that you can remove two dishes from a menu with the same sales profile and whilst one evinces howls of disapproval the other disappears without a murmur. This is because the one that is missed is a favourite, and whilst not always ordered its presence on the menu is crucial to a regular customer who *might* order it if they don't fancy something else – often *their* signature dish.

Chef was disappointed about the smoked salmon, so I taught him my adopted technique when in doubt about anything when opening a restaurant – I write a 'review' . . . like this:

*'One of the most eagerly anticipated openings of the year was the return of Jeremy King to restaurants after the very public falling out with his Investors at "Corbin & King" – owner of The Wolseley amongst others. Especially interesting is that he has chosen to return with a reworking of his first restaurant, from 1981, Le Caprice, now known as Arlington – it seems that Richard Caring hadn't wanted to cede the name. With two years to contemplate what the menu would be, its reveal held us all with bated breath. Imagine the collective sigh of disappointment when smoked salmon leapt out at us from the menu – is that the best he could do?'*

It could now go one of two ways. Either:

'*King really needs to understand that the world of restaurants has changed dramatically since 1981 and he can't rest on his laurels . . .*'

Or:

'*I couldn't resist ordering it and quickly I understood why King had appeared so lazy and conservative – it was simply the best smoked salmon offering I had experienced anywhere, combining first-class produce with superb presentation – this was a dish that spoke volumes of authority and confidence.*'

As I explained to chef – if the latter, then I was good to go . . .

To my relief the menu proved to be a great success in its combination of the old with the new.

# Negotiation

For all that it has been a feature of my life, I hate negotiation, and it has been a source of much discomfort over the years. I was the one who returned to the hotel from a Moroccan souk with a pair of those ubiquitous slippers, chuffed in my reduction from 50 dirham down to 25 only to discover another hotel guest struck a bargain at 10. And even at this level there is a deep feeling of ignominy and dejection! So although now I am perfectly proficient in obtaining discounts, earlier in my career I needed to find some methods to make it more palatable and also not lose sight of the Wildean opinion on 'Knowing the price of everything but the value of nothing'. I didn't want to be a cynic. The other aspect was that I had perceived that there is a very big difference between one-off negotiations and ongoing relationships.

The real breakthrough came prosaically at a time when Le Caprice was just becoming really well known and I found myself sitting in the office opposite a steam pressure-cleaner salesman. These cleaners had just come onto the market and transformed kitchen maintenance, and the ability to deep-clean was revelatory. After a trial, our chef was desperate to acquire one, asking if he could send in the salesman. Of course.

Before he said anything I was scrutinising him and reflecting that I had no idea at all what the machine was worth. Was it £200, £2,000 or £20,000? (remember, this is the 1980s and there is no internet). I am mentally back in the souk and feeling distinctly uncomfortable, but at the same time that experience offered me the solution. 'Now, the price . . .' he began. I interrupted him and said, 'There is no discussion.' He looked at me and I went on, 'You are going to tell me the price and I will pay it.' He raised his eyebrows. 'However, if I find that you have sold it cheaper to anyone else of our level of influence, then not only will I revoke your ability to say that I bought one but also bad-mouth you within the fraternity of peers. You know what is a fair price, so just give me that.'

It worked and it turned out that I had a better price than most.

The question is really about the delicate balance between price and value, and the particular definition of that in the eyes of the recipient.

I was put in mind of this some twenty years later. It was a Sunday lunch at The Wolseley and in comes one of the then investors, along with his son. The son remarked on a tweed suit I was wearing and how he admired it and that he had also liked the previous night's suit, too. 'Do you get them made?' he asked. 'I have to,' I replied, to which his father interrupted, saying, 'How much do you pay?'

'I have no idea,' I said, as much on principle as through ignorance – I am sure there must be aphorisms about gentlemen never knowing what their tailor charges – the only important obligation being to pay their bills, eventually. 'That's ridiculous,' he said. 'And anyway you should come to "us" – we will give you a 50 per cent discount.' (They owned Austin Reed.)

'But I am perfectly happy with my tailor.'

He asked why I would ever turn down a discount.

'Because I have been offered them before, not least by dear Dougie Hayward.' Dougie was a legend in the tailoring world and the inspiration for Michael Caine's 'Alfie' and the character of Harry Pendel in Le Carré's *The Tailor of Panama*. His client list was a who's who of the 60s and 70s (photos of many of whom adorn the walls of Arlington, along with a portrait of Dougie himself), and after he moved his workshop from Pall Mall to a house in Mount Street he held court there with the likes of Alec Guinness, Ralph Lauren and his particularly close group 'The Mayfair Orphan's Club' – Michael Caine, photographer Terry O'Neill, Tramp Club owner Johnny Gold and trichologist Philip Kingsley. Being a Dougie client was considered an honour.

'Years ago he offered me a 50 per cent discount on suits, too, so I gave it a try. But he wouldn't listen to me explaining the vagaries of my six-foot-five frame, so consequently that suit, despite being 50 per cent discounted, cost me £1,500 every time I wore it.'

'How can that be?' he asked.

'Because I only wore it once!'

In truth I had learned about the nature of discounts in a camera shop in New York in the Seventies. The salesman was very good and he knew he had this naïve young man hook, line and sinker before I remembered that someone had told me to be sure to ask for a discount. The conversation went like this.

'Can I have a discount?'

'Of course!' he replied. That was easy I thought and then, on reflection, 'How much?'

'You're a nice English boy and I like you. I want to help. I tell you what I'll do: you tell me how much discount you want,' and, lowering his voice, went on, 'and I will tell you the price.'

Quite.

I stayed with my tailor.

And of course I have since conducted so many negotiations with landlords, suppliers and staff. The essential element for me is fairness. Most of us like to play by the rules and generally play fair, but sometimes you will have dealings with a person playing by their own rules.

I am reminded of an especially tricky situation early in the life of Le Caprice. Chris and I had extricated ourselves from our original partnership with Joseph Ettedgui, but were involved with another man, let's call him Francois, who had acted as an intermediary between us and Joseph, allowing us to continue as operators. However, Francois was now holding us to ransom on the cost of Chris and myself taking full control of the business as he held the 'option' to purchase. He was threatening to sell the option to a known criminal, and it appeared there was nothing I could do. We were fighting with him; the lawyers were fighting with each other; we were fighting with Joseph, our partner, and it seems we were at Francois's mercy.

That is, until we took a new look at the situation. Our agreement with Joseph depended on the rent being paid. So instead of trying to deal with Francois we turned to Joseph and explained a plan. We would withhold the rental money without telling Francois, who would therefore go into default, allowing Joseph to repossess the business – and we would then take over the lease ourselves after a twenty-four-hour hiatus of repossession.

It was risky, but the only way of breaking free. With our hearts in our mouths the lawyers arrived, the seizure notices went up, and Chris and I soon had ownership. Adversity transformed into success and our entire future was secured.

I firmly believe that any problem has a solution if we look at it creatively – but only if we have quelled our fear, which is the enemy of clear thinking. Solutions comes in many forms, though, and the perceived 'good result' is not always the best one.

I will leave the last word to the celebrated American businessman and investor Warren Buffett: 'You can't make a good deal with a bad person.'

Best just to not work with them at all.

# A good lawyer is paramount

While some negotiations I've tackled alone, for many others I've leaned heavily on the expertise of talented lawyers.

I have engaged many lawyers in my time, but the one who saved my life was Ian Rosenblatt who along with his estimable litigation expert Simon Walton held my hand and guided me through the legal maze of my fight with Minor and subsequent machinations. They not only did so expertly but generously as well, and I will be forever grateful. I always felt that it was destiny, as ironically when we met at his house to discuss the loss of my company it was in the house that I had previously lost in divorce – he had purchased it by coincidence. A trusty way to find a good lawyer is often observing who is effective as an adversary's!

When we bought The Ivy, it was Michael Gien of Michael David & Co. who acted for us. My first encounter with Michael had come much earlier, in 1977, when he was recommended to me to handle the conveyancing on a flat I was buying with my then girlfriend. When ready, he called us in to his office and said that he had the papers prepared, but before he would allow us to sign them we had to sign another document. He the slid said document across the table.

'What's this?' I asked.

'It is your agreement on how to handle the sale of the property and contents when you break up.'

'But we don't need this – we are in love and are going to get married.'

'How touching,' he said, 'but I am afraid that unless you sign I'm not going to let you go ahead. I am happy to give you my work gratis to take elsewhere, but I can't with good conscience let either of you go into this unprotected.'

So we signed, and went away moaning about him and how awful

he was and we wouldn't be using him again. But of course, two years later I was back in his office saying, 'Thank you, thank you, thank you.' He had been right and we had indeed separated.

I remember quoting this exchange to my then law firm who advised us on the purchase of The Wolseley.

Of course, it's important not to check out and leave it all to the lawyers. Remember, we are all capable of our own insights – the lawyers are just better trained and more disciplined. My favourite moment was when I was listening to both sides argue about 'warranties'. These come into play when the purchaser discovers that the information supplied by the seller is not proving accurate and it has to be decided in advance what the threshold is of when a purchaser can make a claim. Of course, a purchaser thinks £5k and the seller counters with £500k – the fair figure more likely to be £50k–100k.

Both sides dug in their heels and as the 'costs meter' was running I decided, after a while, to ask the question: 'Ok – let's reverse the situation and roles and tell me what you would be asking for now.' Naturally they fatuously claimed they would expect the same levels, but they got the point and compromised.

One of the toughest negotiations I found myself in was over a new restaurant we were developing that had a tricky freeholder. The story started when our contractors cut into what they thought was a foundation slab only to discover they had got through to the basement – this was due to the owner not supplying the requested plans. The structural engineer said an adhesive was sufficient remedy but wouldn't put it in writing, so we had to 'fess up to the owner, who stopped all works and tried to rip us off by demanding £250k in compensation, saying we had critically damaged his building. I refused, despite my solicitor and QC imploring me to accept as otherwise six months later we could be at stalemate and no work would have been done. All this had been conducted by my financial director in dialogue with the owner through email and there was palpable enmity. The owner was in business with my ex-lawyer and even he couldn't unlock the situation, which was escalating with attendant costs. So I phoned him.

Oh my, he was difficult and wouldn't hear reason. 'I don't know you – how can I trust you?' he asked. I retorted that he did know my lawyer, who had vouched for my integrity, but still he was antagonistic. 'I haven't met you – how can I do business with you?'

'You're right. Where are you? I'm coming to see you.'

And twenty minutes later I was standing at the end of a long room with a large glass-fronted meeting room at the other end, with the whole room turned to look at me because clearly the owner had told them who I was and that I was trouble. He stood up and came towards me, and all I could feel was anger and hatred for what he was doing to me, but as he got closer I felt the anger dissipate for some reason and then he was standing in front of me – scrutinising me.

'Well, Mr King – what are we going to do?'

I looked him in the eye and said: 'We are going to continue to look each other in the eye and I will promise that I will protect your building and then we will shake hands and you will agree to me going back on site and we will put this all behind us . . .'

And he stared into my eyes, it felt like almost into my soul, for what seemed minutes and then took me by the hand and said, 'Ok.'

And the problem was over and an enemy became my friend.

My most significant victory in the courts took place in 2022. In the wake of the Covid pandemic, the insurance conglomerate AXA was refusing to pay out for our loss of trade after we had effectively been locked out of our premises by lockdown restrictions. I was furious about this and determined to fight back, but nobody seemed prepared to take them on – until I found in Jeffrey Gruder KC a barrister who was. Our battle with AXA had potential ramifications for the whole insurance industry, as well as for hospitality, and many people were watching with interest. It was a tense and challenging time, but I was delighted to work with Jeffrey in what was a unprecedented victory that yielded £4.4 million and resulted in the hospitality industry claiming billions of withheld compensation on the strength of our win.

# Anger and conflict

The experience of the loss of the Corbin & King restaurants exemplified the personal defence mechanisms I employ in the face of adversity. These are self-taught, but they have been immensely useful in dealing with bad news or ostensible failure. They are perhaps best exemplified by the moment I categorically realised that I was employing this technique.

I was driving around the streets of Highgate, in North London, looking for a parking space for my old Bristol as I was late for an appointment with an architect. I was tense because of my tardiness and because I was suffering from a back spasm. Impatiently waiting at a T junction for an oncoming Range Rover from my right, I noticed there appeared to be something wrong with the scene – the driver didn't seem to be fully in control. It was signalling to turn into my street but the trajectory was off and it seemed to be going too fast, then I realised it was going to hit me. As it ploughed into the side of my pride and joy, my first thought was: 'Well, it could do with a respray anyway.'

And there I realised my default protection. On re-examining previous big setbacks, bad news, being thwarted, I realised that asking 'where are the positives?' was how I had dealt with and transcended them. Initially losing Le Caprice in early 1982 became a great opportunity and the making of our career – and there were many other examples when I had intuitively exercised positivity over despair. This is crucial. We will all face serious problems and setbacks in our life and we need to find a way for these events to embolden rather than define us.

The incident reinforced for me the value of one of my vows that I had taken a few years before – that I would never swear. The latent aggression of stress and conflict in the restaurant business is legendary – witness the persona Gordon Ramsay developed. The problem is that if too readily used, swearing in, say, a kitchen, can quickly lead to violence, and even if not, the recipients of the tirades are often humiliated, which is unacceptable.

My forswearing of swearing would mean that I would have to articulate my anger, and I found that doing so I would often dissipate the frustration or rage. I reinforced this by offering a fine to every individual who heard me – however many there were present.

The upshot of this is that after I had been hit by the Range Rover, and having crawled out of the passenger door in pain, it was not inconceivable that I would be mad at the driver. But I was determined not to swear. The driver was a young woman who, as I wrote my name down, exclaimed, 'Oh, I thought it was you, Jeremy – you know my father!' Indeed I did. He was a property developer who had used his influence and advice to help me through planning on the property I was having the meeting about. Imagine the ignominy if the driver had reported back to her father that I had sworn at his daughter. Whether our own family or a stranger, everyone in our orbit deserves the same consideration and treatment – and indeed we should treat others in the same way we would like our own children and family treated.

It is clear that most swearing is borne out of anger. Anger itself is the major impediment to finding solutions – and my most-utilised tool to finding a solution is to ask questions. While most problem-solving in a restaurant is about being calm and keeping your voice down, questions are also inordinately effective.

It has evolved in my mind as a series of questions being asked rather than assertions being made. Try it at home. Let's say your child is at the cantankerous age whereby any denial of request can elicit the response 'You don't love me', or 'You don't care about me', or similar. Never argue the toss and find yourself quite legitimately but unsuccessfully trying to prove that your expense on school fees alone should justify your annoyance – just ask the question:

'Do you really believe that?'

And soon you will notice there are innumerable questions that make a point without an assertion which might purely lead to defensiveness.

A favourite of mine is:

'Are you making your issues *my* problem?'

I had a lot of fun one year with the catchphrase 'Deal with it!', which although sounding off-hand was the perfect response to many a moan or complaint, particularly from the staff, because rather than being dismissive is actually implicitly showing a belief in the individual's ability to indeed 'deal with it'.

One of the surefire ways of winning an argument is to relinquish the need to have the other protagonist admit that they were wrong and you are right – even though both sides probably know the truth. The generally male need to be acknowledged as victor often prevents a triumph. It is far better when you see stubbornness replacing logic to 'agree to disagree' and then just watch to see whether your adversary changes their behaviour anyway. Countless times I have stood between an aggressive, demanding customer and their goal and it is fascinating how often a thwarted guest turns to aggression and insults. The lesson is never to argue, just to ask a question in return or to ignore.

A customer who, for instance, has been asked to leave will often lash out, saying such things as 'This restaurant is terrible anyway, you don't know what you are doing, you run this so badly it will close soon anyway, etc.' Now, I might well feel that I am within my rights to dispute these assertions, but to what end? My typical response is always, 'Be that as it may, you are still leaving,' which is inordinately effective. I am fortunate that proprietorial presence has made our restaurants the least-confrontational I have ever encountered. However, over the years I have been punched, had a beer stein thrown in my face, been shouted at and threatened, but I am fortunate to have a non-excitable pulse and the perspicacity to speak quietly in adversity. I have removed tables from in front of aggressors, whispered in their ears what will happen if they carry on with their behaviour, gently goaded the truly aggressive by getting too close until they assault me, thus giving us reason to either kick them out or even, if necessary, call the police – but never, ever shouted, as that would legitimise escalation.

As a leader it is crucial that we are seen by our staff and customers to be consistent and dependable – whilst at the same time not being stubborn or incapable of adaptability. When faced with a dilemma as to how to react to a situation, I always recommend reverting to consistency and behaviour that we can defend or be proud of. I have experienced many such lessons but probably the toughest revolve around upsetting people whilst retaining integrity. Probably the one occasion on which I wistfully regret I had to maintain consistency was after the arrival of Andy Warhol at Le Caprice in the 1980s. He took out his camera, of course, and started photographing his group and the restaurant. Naturally this was great for the restaurant, but we were known for a 'No photography' rule and I felt the eyes of both the staff and customers trained on my reaction to this solecism. Of course, they then enjoyed watching as I bent down to ask Warhol to refrain and see what his reaction would be. Well, he smiled and acceded readily after I explained that the rule was actually made to protect people like himself. Of course I am sad that the photos don't exist, but I don't regret my intervention, as the story travelled and the staff appreciated the principle.

By way of contrast I remember the reaction of the staff at a high-profile restaurant that had opened just as the ban on smoking in restaurants had been implemented. One of the guests was Philip Green, then at the height of his pomp. When he lit up a cigarette the staff were in a quandary as to what to do, so the owner was approached by the manager and asked what he should do. 'Get him an ashtray!' was the response. So the indulgence was made – but at the cost of respect and ongoing contempt of the staff.

Short term gain – long term loss.

In brief, solving problems and dealing with adversity is rarely achieved through swearing, anger, negativity and aggression. When I was in the depths of my fights with my last investor, and I was in danger of losing the restaurants, I realised that the confrontations and conflict were getting to me so much that I took the unusual step of giving myself a good talking to. Much to my own surprise, I sat down with a metaphorical wagging finger and told myself very firmly, out loud, 'When it comes to business you will never, ever allow anyone or anything to upset you ever again.' Strangely enough, it worked, and serenity pervaded my thoughts – so much so that my solicitor asked me in the height of the conflict: 'How do you remain so calm?'

I explained the effectiveness of my recent self-admonition. He raised an eyebrow in response, so I further qualified it by saying, 'and because you are so good at getting upset on my behalf!'

# Empathy

How often in life do we create problems by only seeing situations from our point of view? It should be the role of the restaurateur and operatives to see beyond the prima facie evidence of perhaps bad behaviour, disagreement and conflict, and instead of reacting negatively to find it in ourselves to be positive. I try to teach this using an example of an imaginary pair of couples out for dinner on a Saturday night. If it appears judgemental, or stereotypical, please forgive me, but frankly it is entirely borne out of observation.

This is my teaching example.

You are the lead maître d'hôtel. It is a busy Saturday night at The Wolseley, let's say at 8.53 p.m. And in through the door comes a couple who don't look particularly happy. On welcoming them you ask for the reservation name and they say: 'Smith – for four at 9 p.m.' You explain that they are the first to arrive (and you notice the shared look, frown and raise of the eyebrows), that the table isn't quite ready and would they like to have a drink in the bar while waiting. They are a little terse in saying 'No thank you – we will wait here for the Smiths.'

A few minutes past 9 p.m., there comes through the door a slightly harassed woman who apologises to the waiting couple and then repeats 'Smith – four at 9 p.m. – can we sit down now?' It's a command rather than a request and you apologise and say that you are running a little late and could you arrange a drink for them and all you receive in reply is a rather dismissive tut and she moves to the other couple, apologising for her lateness. It's not going well so far.

At approximately 9.07 p.m. an out-of-breath and red-faced man clatters through the door and with a quick glance at the other three says very abruptly: 'The name is Smith – four at 9 p.m. – why can't we sit down?' And as you begin to apologise he starts shouting, 'Why the hell is the table not ready? What's the point of booking if you are so bleeding inefficient that you can't have it ready? This is ridiculous – get me the manager right away!'

And you are now angry, with all your hackles up, and the last thing you want to do is accede to this bully . . . This is turning into a confrontation.

But wait. Time out. Let's run the clock back and see the situation from another perspective.

Now imagine we are in the Smiths' car and it is 8.50 p.m. They are on the way to meet the Browns for their monthly dinner in the West End. They have been doing this since they first met and bonded when their kids attended the same primary school – a time when the parents were as apprehensive as the children and it was reassuring to be able to discuss uncertainties with another set of parents. Truth is, the kids have now gone to different secondary schools and although the parents have also drifted apart neither couple feels they can stop the monthly ritual and they are locked in to the unwanted obligation. Colin and Carol Smith, who have been married the best part of twenty years, have also drifted apart and it is fair to say they don't really like each other.

Tonight, Colin would be happier at home with a bottle of wine anticipating *Match of the Day* on TV.

Meanwhile, Carol's frustration with what can only be described as a recalcitrant and boorish husband is boiling over, and as they drive, she is making some justifiable requests regarding the evening.

'And can you not drink so much this evening? It makes me so nervous when you are driving – I really don't understand why you insist on bringing the car when the tube would have been easier and frankly quicker. Yet again we are going to be late and you know how they are always early. And can you please not tell those jokes, nobody likes them and they are embarrassing – particularly when you repeat them.'

Colin is now white-knuckled at the wheel. He is not taking that space for anything and insists on pressing on to get closer. Piccadilly is both jammed and without any parking spaces so Carol insists she will get out as 'You know they will be there already.' After another five minutes jammed in traffic Colin eventually effectively dumps the car on a double line, anticipating the censure the resultant ticket will elicit, and runs to the restaurant.

So when he comes through the door he is stressed and frustrated and needs to take that out on someone. Whilst it should be in the form of stopping this charade with the Browns and having a heart to heart with his wife, inevitably it is easier to take it out on you.

You cannot allow this to happen. Remember my rule: 'Don't let someone's issues become your problem.' However, you don't 'punish' them – you must spoil them, even if it goes against every instinct. And if they go off on a rant or diatribe you know you have my backing to say, 'We are not going to honour your reservation.' Because I have shown you how to do this and you have heard me say to aggressive, apoplectic customers that we won't take it any further and are refusing the reservation. I see no point having them in the restaurant in order to take their frustrations out on my staff.

Normally, at this point, their partner calms them down – and *then* our real work begins. We have to transform them, show the benefits of love and mutual respect and try to ensure that they leave happy, hopefully thinking about their friendships, and indeed marriage.

# Conforming

I am ostensibly and apparently a rather traditional and formal person in so many ways, but at the same time I am fundamentally a closet contrarian. And that is because I am determined to be what I want to be rather than what someone else dictates or feels they can determine. Having said that, the dichotomy in me is that I have written earlier about my dislike of dress code, and yet if an invitation calls for 'Black Tie' I will certainly adhere and you won't find me trying to jazz it up for the sake of garnering attention (I mean, what other reason can there be for the self-conscious tropes of long ties, black shirts, etc.?). There is respect, and there is convention, and I wondered where my dilemmas and unpredictability stem from. Two stories from 1973 – the year I arrived in London and started my job in merchant banking – illustrate my feelings on the matter.

It was a few months before my arrival that the head of personnel had looked at me and said: 'If we give you this job you will have to get rid of the beard.'

'Why?' I replied.

'No one trusts a man with a beard in the City,' came the reply.

To which I cheekily retorted: 'Surely that can't be true. Isn't that the same judgement that people used to make about anyone wearing suede shoes? And wouldn't it be fair to say that if we were here in the 1870s rather than 1970s you would be saying, 'No one trusts a man *without* a beard?'

Point of the story is that I kept the beard, much to the chagrin of the bank, and yet when I did decide to remove it no one even noticed! (Other than the floor commissionaire from Crystal Palace.) It really annoyed me and stayed with me in a mist of resentment and confusion.

But the moment when I really learned the lesson of conformity and individuality was at the Rainbow Theatre, Finsbury Park, in April 1973 during a Captain Beefheart concert. Now 'The Captain' (real name, Don Van Vliet) was esoteric and one of the poster boys of the psychedelic movement of West Coast America – his many albums included the almost unfathomable *Trout Mask Replica*, and I was a devotee. My heroes in the changing line-up of his Magic Band included Rockette Morton, Zoot Horn Rollo, Antennae Jimmy Semens. I had introduced my brother, Pete, to the music and he in turn was similarly obsessed and had acquired the tickets to this concert.

My plan to go home and change out of my City suit was thwarted by having to stay late at the office, so to my massive shame I joined my embarrassed brother in the queue to get in wearing a grey double-breasted suit (with a light purple stripe), a mauve shirt and matching tie – surprisingly fashionable in some milieu, but not for a Beefheart concert. I was surrounded by the majority of concertgoers wearing the 'alternative' uniform of 'loon pants', tie-dye T-shirts and Afghan coats – if you were really cool even trademark Beefheart-coloured top hats.

And I was in a boring suit. The contemptuous looks, open jeering and derision made me want to leave, but Pete persuaded me to stay, and with hunched shoulders I shuffled in, humiliated.

Let me hand over to someone else at the concert – reviewer 'Benjamin Horrendous'.

*'The concert started with Rockette Morton with an electric toaster strapped on his head. He said, "Good evening. My name is Rockette Morton. I've just come on to do a toast." Then he leapt into the air and played a short free form solo. He went into the riff from "Mirror Man" and the band joined in.*

*Beefheart came on playing the harp and exhorting everyone to their feet. Hundreds of people left their seats and ran to the front of the stage. It was a brilliant gig.'*

What he doesn't mention is that Rockette Morton walked onto that stage incomprehensibly dressed in a grey suit with a mauve shirt – completely unexpected and out of character. And suddenly the morose Jeremy King was a cult hero garnering admiring looks and intense kudos. After the concert had finished people shook my hand, congratulated me and asked whether I was a friend of the band.

That taught me a great deal about appearances and being accepted.

CODA: In 1986 I am talking to Leslie Waddington, one of the great gallerists and a true supporter and friend of Le Caprice, who is asking for a large table for a post-opening dinner for a new artist he has taken on. He is lamenting the fact that he doesn't know how to talk to this man and has only taken him on at the behest of probably the most-lauded American artist of the time, Julian Schnabel. Leslie is particularly apprehensive about the lunch the next day with this rather wild man. 'Who is he?' I ask, and he says the name is Don Van Vliet.

'Don Van Vliet!' I exclaim. 'You mean Captain Beefheart?' I say excitedly, and Leslie believes that's right, 'Apparently he's a bit of a rock star.' And as I start to explain who he is and his role in my schooldays and beyond, Leslie interrupts me, saying, 'I don't know what you might be doing next Thursday but whatever it is please cancel – you are joining us at Mr Chow.'

And so I did. Leslie and Clodagh Waddington scurried away as soon as was respectable and they left me with my hero for the rest of the afternoon. And what an afternoon. Don wanted to buy some British-style slippers and was entranced by the oldest men's shoe shop, Trickers, in Jermyn Street, and even more so when I bought him a pair with a fox embroidered on them – his favourite animal.

I offered him a lift to his hotel in Knightsbridge. As we walked to collect my car from under Le Caprice he talked of his (surprising) love of British cars and that his favourite was one called a 'Bristol', which he had seen in a showroom and rarely elsewhere. I left him to await me bringing out the car and I still treasure the look on his face when he realised I was driving . . . a Bristol.

They say never meet your heroes. I disagree.

*First car*

*Current car*

# Circumspection

For someone who professes to have enjoyed risk, circumspection is an unlikely title for a chapter in this book, however, the clue is in the definition:

*Careful to consider all circumstances and possible consequences.*

Ignore at your peril – as I learned the hard way.

An old friend is the actress Caroline Quentin, whom I got to know at Le Caprice and developed the friendship as The Ivy opened. I adored her because she would happily and readily engage in banter and abuse and was quick to tease with her razor-sharp wit and intelligence.

It was after she had tried to humiliate me in the restaurant one time that I decided to play a prank on her. The opportunity came because she was garnering a lot of attention when she starred in the TV series *Men Behaving Badly*. I left a voicemail for her, on a Saturday evening, saying in a disguised and seedy accent:

"Ello, Ms Quentin – this is Jerry Le Roi from the *News of the World*, wondering whether you had any further comment on our article about you tomorrow?'

I figured she would recognise my voice, despite disguise, and certainly deduce that 'Jerry Le Roi' was actually 'Jeremy the King'. But she didn't and duly raced down to Leicester Square to find the paper.

This was pre-internet times and advance copies of the papers could be found there at midnight. Apparently she ended up scouring the *News of the World* several times and then bought all the others just in case. When she listened to the message again it finally dawned on her who 'Jerry Le Roi' actually was and was soon on the phone with abuse and threats – 'I will get you back, you bastard'!

So I was very watchful in order not be caught out, but after a few

*Caroline Quentin*

weeks nothing had happened and so I let my guard down somewhat. However not so much that I was going to let a transparent effort by her to get through. My assistant told me one morning that there was a man with an unusual voice on the phone, calling himself the Count de Saint Quentin, trying to get a table for New Year's Eve.

'Put him through,' I said – thinking, this will be fun.

And I was listening to a hesitating, high-pitched voice:

'Oh, hello, Mr King, I am sorry to trouble you but I would be terribly grateful if I could come to The Ivy with a companion on New Year's Eve. Would that be at all possible?'

'In your dreams!' was my reply to Caroline the Count. 'Have you mispronounced the title? Why on earth would I ever want you to be in my restaurant – go and find something more appropriate.' (I was enjoying this.)

'Well, I am sure you are busy, but I do rather like The Ivy and my friend was keen to try.'

'Tough,' I continued. 'Not on my watch.'

'That's a terrible shame,' came their reply.

'Deal with it,' was mine, and then, 'oh come on, Quentin: enough of this silly voice – you are not going to fool me.'

And then there was silence until they said, 'I am sorry, I don't understand.'

Suddenly a horrible realisation dawned on me: this wasn't Caroline, it was in fact the Comte de Saint Quentin.

'I am so terribly sorry – I thought I was talking to someone else.'

'I did think your tone was rather strange and aggressive.'

'Of course you can have a table.'

Caroline howled with laughter when I told her and enjoyed that she had exacted her revenge. And I had learned that before we ever say anything to anyone to be sure we are fully briefed, researched and informed. That we must never trust the surprise caller, double-check who we are sending a message to, terminate calls properly, hesitate before we 'reply all' and now, with the AI transcription of calls and meetings, find out who is on the distribution list and remember that if someone leaves the meeting the absentee will still get the transcription if they are discussed after departure.

# Beware of false economy

Too much of 'good business' nowadays is predicated by cutting costs. I have had many a conversation with managers about how I am keen never to waste money, but at the same time I am only prepared to cut costs if there is no (or negligible) impact on customers.

To that end, I tell the story from Le Caprice, back in the days when people still smoked. One afternoon Chris checked the restrooms downstairs and returned to let the Head Waiter know that there were no ashtrays in either.

'Oh, we haven't replaced them yet.'

'How do you mean "replaced"?'

'Well, in every service they are taken.'

'What, all of them?'

'Yes, all four of them. And of an evening, often twice . . .'

The ashtrays were plain, small, white affairs, but they were badged with 'Le Caprice'.

Chris duly set off to John Lewis to buy two very large, heavy and theft-proof glass ashtrays. Very pragmatic and sensible thinking. Problem solved – and how much consequently saved?

Well, conservatively, let's say twelve ashtrays a day, which is over 4,000 a year and – at today's prices – the best part of £25,000 saved with no detriment to customer experience. In truth the new ones looked more appropriate than our little ones. Everyone was happy.

Until I began to wonder whether there was a cost to the saving. There would no longer be 4,000 new adverts each year placed in good homes across the world, nor acting as a reminder to the thief to return it to the restaurant (maybe a little guilt involved here?) – and depriving them of showing to their friends and visitors that they frequented a fashionable London restaurant.

That's a very valuable marketing campaign suddenly cut short.

It's not the obvious we must examine, but the lateral possibilities. As restaurateurs we try to make a visit memorable for the food, service and environment – and when these all coalesce into a happy experience, people often do want a memento. So, remember that cancelling the expense of making, for example, elegant matchboxes might be a good cost saver, but it also deprives, not least of a sense of generosity. I am always looking for ways for people to feel that they are experiencing that; the limoncello moment in an Italian restaurant is a perfect example.

In all walks of life and business I carry the credo: when you think you have done enough, do a little bit more.

A final coda regarding ashtrays: their need having been obviated threatens an earlier termination to my career. One of the most charming sights in European family run restaurants was that of an elderly man shuffling between the tables sharing a moment with long-standing clientele who regard him with affection as he changes the ashtrays. This would inevitably be the old proprietor, now too infirm and forgetful to fulfil a meaningful role in the restaurant other than as a host. The ashtrays facilitate his enduring contact with customers.

# Overlooking your greatest asset

By now perhaps you won't be surprised when I say that the asset most often and foolishly overlooked within our industry is the staff – or not inappropriately now referred to as 'talent'. And the greatest talent is not necessarily the most adept, dextrous, accurate, efficient and effective. I am more interested in attitude, warmth, aura and charisma – the trade skills can be taught.

But how do we find this talent? In hospitality there are ways of gleaning in seconds information that an hour of interview won't reveal. Anton Mosimann (previously head chef of The Dorchester) would ask a candidate to carry a pot to the dishwash, claiming he could tell from the way they did it whether they were comfortable in a kitchen. My personal favourite is to ask a potential waiter/server to pick up three plates off a table – to an experienced waiter it is natural, whereas the charlatan will be flummoxed. (The technique is to put the first plate into the left hand leaving the little finger to support the second one resting on the wrist whilst picking up the third with the right.)

Like any industry, the restaurant world is rife with poaching, but it is not a practice I subscribe to. My philosophy is that if I am a good-enough employer, and can be seen to truly care for the staff, then eventually people will come to me or will be recommended, and I won't have to 'poach'.

After Covid and Brexit there has been a crisis not in obtaining staff but particularly talented staff, and then keeping them when they are being showered with offers. However, it is more than just money that endures as the guardian of your staff: it is essential that they are trained, trusted, valued and respected, and their dignity and value transcends indulging a high-spending customer who treats them as servants.

When I opened The Park we were actually fortunate enough to be able to draw wonderful staff but we allowed for attrition so we over-hired – to my immense gratification we had too many and actually needed to lend some to other restaurants!

In the world of restaurants I have often persuaded staff to change their career path – for instance, Kitchen to Floor or vice versa – or even leave the business altogether to pursue their real dreams. It might seem foolish to create an unnecessary vacancy, and in truth I have irritated many a head chef or manager by depriving them of a talent, but I explain that it will be repaid in goodwill and even karma. I particularly upset the head chef at The Ivy in the Nineties when the Australian government announced they would give a visa to anyone under twenty-five who would like to go there for eighteen months with the opportunity of extending. I had HR draw up a list of everyone under twenty-five and spoke to them personally about it – it was too good an opportunity for them to miss, I felt. As the chef expressed annoyance, I reasoned with him that many would return, hopefully grateful for the experience, and whilst they were in Australia they would extol the virtues of a company that put the employee first and encourage them to join if they went to London.

The more we encourage our staff to find their true vocation the greater the chance of happiness. A company can manage without any individual, including the CEO, but that individual only has one life and maybe only one career, so we have a responsibility to help them succeed.

Around the time we were opening The Delaunay, at the end of 2011, with Brasserie Zédel and Colbert to follow in quick succession, Chris decided to pull back from a more full-time role and was keen that I took sole control, although he would still come in part-time. This acted as a catalyst for me thinking about how the company should now be organised. One of the steps I took was to seek advice from customers who ran larger businesses, including the CEO of advertising agency M&C Saatchi, David Kershaw.

On interviewing him, I asked how he managed to control five-strong founder partners, over twenty subsidiary agencies and well over 2,000 staff.

'It's all about delegation.'

'Oh come on, David, that's what people always say, but what does that actually mean?'

'I assume you know the first rule of delegation then?'

'I don't know. I didn't know there was a set of rules about delegation. Tell me then.' And he came out with this:

'You must never, ever, *ever* delegate *anything* whatsoever at all to *anyone* whatsoever unless you have complete and utter confidence in their ability to successfully carry out the task you have delegated. Simple as that.'

And I realised I wasn't following the first rule, and I was feeling the consequences. Let's not set people up to fail. For me, the crucial element is to get good, decent people appointed and to 'play them in position' – you wouldn't sign David Beckham and put him in goal.

I learned this the hard way, having watched too often a great senior chef de partie (senior chef on a section of the stoves) being turned into an inadequate sous chef (kitchen manager), just because they were the next in line in terms of longevity or seniority. What I persuade my head chefs to do in these situations is to give the individual the title, give them the pay rise, but keep them on the stoves.

I remember once castigating the head of food and beverage at the Tate Gallery in the Nineties because, having poached one of my sous chefs as his head chef – having assumed that if they were sous chef at The Ivy the move to head chef would be easy – he then complained to me that the chef wasn't very good. I told him I could have told him that readily if he had called me. The guy was an excellent producer of food under pressure but couldn't plan, lead, create a menu or understand the business elements to save his life. What I castigated him about was the ridiculousness that he would entrust a stranger with 60 per cent of his revenue – running into millions of pounds – and yet wouldn't invest 4p to check his references and discover whether that was a good move or not.

We all have strengths and weaknesses, and our job as managers is to recognise the talent and strength and play up to them in order to extract the best performance.

An experience common to many restaurateurs is that of having friends and acquaintances offload their children onto us for work experience. (My own children were no exception: each proudly cite their times in the restaurants as part of their CV, which is a great step forward from the days when there was stigma about working in hospitality.)

My favourite experience of this was when a frustrated friend and parent asked me to give his son a job: 'Any job, it can be washing dishes if that is all you have – his mother is going crazy because he lies in bed till 3 p.m. and then does nothing, is interested in nothing and is completely listless.'

To which I replied, 'Absolutely not.'

The father was more than a little surprised by this because he considered it not too much of an imposition on a good friend, especially as he wasn't somebody in my interest to offend or disappoint. However, I knew what the background was. The fallout of a difficult divorce had been exacerbated by a troubled school career on account of the son's dyslexia and he had moved schools often accordingly. There was an inevitable drop in self-esteem. I went on to explain to the father that acceding to what was requested would break his son and make him feel worthless. However, what I was prepared to do was teach him a profession that transcended his dyslexia and give him the ability to travel the world and discover his true worth – as a barista. But only if the son was prepared to apply for and secure the role himself, volunteer for preliminary training, and promise consistent attendance. To his credit he took on the challenge, excelled at it, and found his smile again. Soon afterwards, in 2011, we opened The Delauney in Aldwych, another Grand Café, very much a kindred operation to The Wolseley – it was also named for a car, in this case the Delaunay-Belleville – but it generated a greater theatrical following. The son was on the staff from the beginning, winning the award for 'Employee of the Month'. His father spoke glowingly of the transformation and how his mother couldn't believe that he was coping with the early starts, looking after his uniform cleaning, tidying his room – an unconscionable turnaround. 'And to his mother's delight she can tell her friends he is training as a barrister!'

We all need to find our own purpose in life and not have it ordained or taken on through obligation. And whether we are parents or employers, it's important to remember as much.

As employers, our responsibility for our staff endures into older age. I am shocked at how many companies feel that staff have a 'best-by date' and offload their older staff often at the time of their greatest potential contribution. Many in my industry were surprised when I started a campaign to hire staff over the age of fifty. This initiative was borne out of experiences I had in the USA which convinced me of the wasted talent in this age group.

My wife Lauren and I had arrived at a restaurant in New Orleans – her home city – and were trying a newly arrived trendy restaurant called Pêche. We had been sat and attended to by a young woman, probably in her early twenties – perfectly pleasant but somewhat going through the motions, and clearly her mind was on an alternative career. The table wasn't great, so when a booth freed up we asked if we could move, and this necessitated a change of server. We relocated and realised that the quite large man well into his fifties was approaching us. Was he an owner, manager? No – our waiter. And the moment he spoke, we melted; he immediately conveyed a wealth of knowledge and more importantly a desire to look after us and ensure we enjoyed the restaurant. And he did, and then later explained that he had previously been in tech but had been given early retirement, which meant that he could pursue his real interest – restaurants. The important aspect is that he was more stable financially, in accommodation, not more interested in clubbing and socialising than serving and was the consummate guide through an inspired restaurant.

It was a week later, in New York, that I sat down at the bar of Stephen Starr's then new restaurant Upland and another fifty-year+ server who was behind the bar said to me, 'Let me think – I reckon a Belvedere Martini straight up with a twist is what you want' – he was right. And as we talked I learned that he was a youthful fifty-five-year-old and discovered he had declined the oft-offered chance of promotion. 'Why do I want to sit in an office doing ordering, rotas and organising when I can be with people?'

It convinced me that this was the way to go, and the more the initiative was publicised the more I got asked to speak to groups of employers – especially post-Brexit – about the possibilities. I also talked about how people could offset the loss of female staff, especially in the kitchen, because of maternity leave, and how mothers could easily be brought back into the industry if we just changed our hours once their children started to attend school. The time we needed the help was when the kids were there.

When I started, the finding of staff was always a 'buyers' market', whereas now it is firmly a sellers' one. Unless we adapt to what these sort of shifts mean, then we die.

# Being a better restaurateur

After losing control of what is now known as the Wolseley Hospitality Group, I found myself with time to reflect on five decades working in restaurants. So when I announced my return to the restaurant business, via a newsletter to friends and customers, it was with the following words:

*'Oh how I have missed you. It has been a long time, but hopefully you will experience the benefits of my enforced sojourn and what I have learned in my time away. I am determined to be a better restaurateur, employer and friend – and I look forward to seeing you.'*

One of the most important insights to have emerged from that time off was about my role as an employer. What I see now more clearly than ever is that the more I show belief in my staff the greater they become. If I believe that they are all embryonic head chefs and restaurateurs, should they want to be, then the more proprietorial they become and the better the customer experience.

Love and humour also come into play.

One of the most beneficial and educational passages of time came to me while observing my daughter Margot going through the trials and tribulations of opening a bar, in December 2024, in the West Village in New York. It is not her profession, but despite this she managed to excel at it, while still excelling in her day job. She had met her business partner-to-be, Emmet McDermott, on what was meant to be a date, but they soon realised that their real shared desire was to open a bar for their contemporaries. Having found a fascinating old site, that of the historic Downtown Gallery on West 13th Street, they put together an impressive team to design, conceive and operate the place under the name 'People's'.

Margot asked me: 'I assume it's fine for me to seek your advice at times?'

To her surprise my answer was 'no'. Followed by the assertion that they could *both* come to me and therefore avoid the dangers of early partnership fracture that the 'My dad says . . .' assertions would have likely caused. They did a great job with the creation of People's, and it was an interesting revelation that the biggest need for counsel was in the area of staff and customer dealings.

Come the opening, Margot and her partner Emmett asked for some guidance on what to say to the staff on opening night. I suggested they emphasise the need for camaraderie, mutual support, no recriminations, good communication – and understanding just how essential humour was. That asking for help was a sign of strength rather than weakness.

When I asked how it had gone, they said the words were useful. 'In what way?' I asked.

Margot explained that halfway through a hectic evening she was tapped on the shoulder by the lady running the cloakroom. This was a makeshift affair because it was in the basement that had just dried out from a flood, the water muddy because of a dirt floor, and they hadn't had time to spruce it up.

'Margot. You know you said we shouldn't hesitate to ask for help? I need help . . .'

And she took Margot downstairs to reveal that the temporary coat rack had collapsed and not only cast all the coats onto a dirty floor but had lost the 'tags' at the same time. It was not going to be possible to bring the guests down to identify their dirty coats – too embarrassing.

'What did you do?' I asked, and she explained they somehow got through but not before they had laughed and continued with a smile on their faces. Their whole-staff ethos led to them not losing a single member of staff in the first month – which must be unique for an opening. It is an old truism that the more you look after your staff the better they will look after the customers.

A couple of months later Margot was due to phone me before going to an event at a new venue that she simply had to attend. I received a text: 'Problem – will have to speak later.'

When we did, she was in a cab telling me that she had received a call from People's telling her all the electricity had gone. Her first reaction was that candlelight was not a problem but quickly realised that the lack of refrigeration, air-conditioning, internet, credit card machines etc., would be much more so, and then the reminder that the pump safeguarding against further flooding necessarily compromised at another level.

'Are you on the way over there?' I asked, and she explained she wasn't: there was nothing she could do and all that she could do had already been done, so she was going to the event.

'I am proud of you,' I said – and refrained from following with 'Welcome to Hospitality.'

It is essential that we relax into tense situations, maintain our humour and perspective and delegate . . .

As for myself? I learned from watching Emmet and Margot that the kinder, fonder, understanding and forgiving I am to staff the greater they become. It is all very different than it was fifty years ago, but in order to stay young, enthused and energised we must constantly change our habits and methods.

We have to fully embrace that this is a new world in employment – on all levels. We truly have to make our staff feel valued and secure, and it is significant that as I write there is a new acknowledgement of how badly women have been treated, occasioned by a piece when a chef claimed they hadn't witnessed sexism in restaurateuring – a situation that couldn't be further from the truth. Even the environment is important, and I have long eschewed the prevailing attitude that 'enough is enough'. If staff are serving in good environments then their own spaces must have the same consideration. I have always believed that just as customers enjoy paintings, prints etc., so will staff, and the disparity between 'Front of House' and 'Back of House' is iniquitous. The benefit of me taking time out meant I could return with greater insight and understanding. At The Park we were struggling to make the staff accommodation work, and the architect and team were incredulous that I rented a further 1,000 square feet for greater comfort. Unquestionably, the more we concentrate on humanity, rather than remain preoccupied with profitability, the greater the ultimate gain.

# The changing face of restaurateuring

## Social and general media

When I told my colleagues in 2012 that we were going to use social media for the opening of Brasserie Zédel, they were in shock. For good reason: for the previous thirty years we had eschewed interviews, features, articles and had completely relied on goodwill and word of mouth.

But remembering Prince Tancredi – 'For things to remain the same, everything has to change' – we had to confront that communications were evolving, demographics changing, and with Zédel we were creating a younger person's 'People's Palace' and we needed to be able to talk to all our target audiences.

We had already seen The Wolseley feature on social media and, as far as I was concerned, it allowed us to hear what was being said in the pubs, restaurants, offices and dining rooms of so many people, and it could be enlightening.

I am a great believer that when someone metaphorically throws a knife, fires a bullet or hurls a spear, we must see the message on that missile but ensure that it doesn't get through and injure us. We all need a shell to protect ourselves from the barbs and slings of an adversary. For many years, I was too pervious; I eventually came to see that I was allowing everything thrown at me to penetrate and hurt. If we have a protective shield, we can stay calm, reasoned and introspective, and, having read the hurtful message, ask ourselves whether it is actually true.

These days, if I'm the subject of criticism I take it as an opportunity to examine myself. And it is well worth remembering that, so often, when someone points a finger at you, three are pointing back at themselves. Projection is truly a powerful thing.

When it comes to publicising our restaurants, I still believe in the 'narrowcast' rather than the 'broadcast', and that whatever media we choose we must recognise the potential for enhancing our reputation – as long as we don't get smug or arrogant about it, nor imagine that social media in itself can make a restaurant successful. We still need to get the fundamentals right. Style and class still have a dominating role in all that we do.

## Tipping

In hospitality a lot of money passes between customers and staff on a transactional basis – and that can lead to problems. I do not like the whole nature of tipping as exemplified particularly in New York nowadays, whereby your credit card payment machine will prompt you with a request as to whether you would like to leave 22, 25 or 30 per cent! The tipping issue has become even more prevalent with self-service coffee shops expecting restaurant-service levels of tipping and online shopping expecting contributions to the staff. In the US customers are more and more frequently being followed into the street by remonstrating staff outraged by more-than-generous tips.

Tipping is for when a customer might want to give a gratuity for particularly good service, but I can't bear the expectation and just wish we could build the gratuity into the menu price. In the UK there is a good reason not to, sadly, because of our tax structure. In order to get the remuneration to a member of staff it would mean at least 50 per cent of it would be redirected to His Majesty's Government in the form of VAT, Income Tax and National Insurance, whereas within the current system only Income Tax at a much lower rate is due.

And this is the flaw in the assertion 'just pay your staff properly', which could only be achieved with large pricing rises to the customer's detriment. I was always so admiring of Danny Meyer in New York when he attempted to deliver on his maxim of 'Hospitality Included' – in every sense. But having taken the bold step to include tipping in the prices, he sadly was forced to revert to the prevailing system. Oh how I wish government would intervene, especially as in the UK the government tried to avoid paying full levels of furlough during the pandemic, claiming they had no obligation to reimburse lost tips although they had been happy to tax them!

If we are to break away from the perceived stigma of working in restaurants, it is critical that the restaurateur charges appropriately and in turn rewards the staff. This rather grubby and suspect transaction between customer and server is demeaning and makes it hard to ensure both chefs and floor staff are properly remunerated.

Do you tip when you collect your dry cleaning, or at the supermarket? Buy a ticket, pay your cleaner, accept your Amazon delivery? Any number of examples point to this all being so wrong. Of course there are many vagaries between industries and the different customs of recognition, and I often smile when I see the credits run on a film, imagining what it would be like if we credited everyone working in the restaurant on the menu!

Occasionally the issue of tipping can involve a clash of cultures, which requires a certain tact and sensitivity to resolve.

In the early Eighties I was once put in a difficult position at Le Caprice when I was saying goodbye to the son of the Prime Minister of Bahrain – a sophisticated and educated young man who I liked a great deal. As he left he reached out his hand to shake mine – or so I thought – because as our hands met I felt the unmistakable presence of a bank note, which a glance revealed as a new £50 note – quite a lot of money in those days. As he went to withdraw his hand I held on to it and said:

'Please, that's very generous of you but I can't accept.'

'Please do,' he said.

'It's really not necessary,' I replied.

'Please accept it from me.'

'I really can't – it's not appropriate.'

We are in a stand-off and I realise that I am going to offend him if I don't accept and he realises that I will be offended if he insists. What to do? His innate understanding of saving face saved the day.

'Please accept – it's not for you,' he said, looking into my eyes.

'You mean it is for the staff?' I ask.

'No,' he responded. 'It's for your children.'

'But I don't have any children.'

'You will.' And with that he had saved the situation and spared our mutual discomfort.

# 'Dynamic Pricing' – or as I like to call it, 'Gouging'

Oh, how I hate that term. It is the scourge of hospitality – or certainly one of the biggest. It is a term that is coming into more common parlance. Whilst, in part, I understand it, I also feel it's too often the most cynical and inhospitable device used by the so-called hospitality industry.

Dynamic pricing refers to the practice whereby a hotel or airline will quote you a price depending on the 'market'. It is an accepted economic principle of supply and demand when based on commodities, but it makes no allowance for some of the more fundamental human experiences.

I sincerely believe that as humans we thrive on loyalty and ritual. When we travel regularly we prefer to use our favourite airline, stay at our usual hotel, where we are known, and whether home or away eat at restaurants where we are recognised and valued.

If it all becomes about the price, our ability to develop loyalty or become a 'regular' is challenged and with that the anxiety of the unknown. By way of example: both my daughters went to university in the United States. Inevitably I would receive calls along the lines of, 'Can I come home for Spring break?' and of course I would say 'yes' and reckon that if I was lucky the economy flight ticket cost at that time would be £350 return, but I had to allow for up to £750. I took the rough with the smooth and understood the variance. That is until our regular airline, British Airways, quoted £1,500 to one of the children for a return. I couldn't say 'don't come', so I asked her to look at other carriers, and I think it was Air New Zealand that came up with a £600 ticket and were also revealed to have a better cabin and facilities. BA might have enjoyed a short-term gain with the higher prices, but they experienced a long-term loss because the spell was broken; the tie of loyalty severed, and we always looked to the Airline Aggregators from then on.

It is the same with hotels. When I opened The Beaumont Hotel I used to be pressured by my management to dynamically price, but I didn't want to – for the same reasons as my airline experiences. I wanted my guests to unhesitatingly answer when asked the question: 'Where do you stay in London?' as 'The Beaumont'. And that would remain the case if I wasn't greedy and gave them service and a welcome beyond that of most five-star hotels. Everyone understands a variance between low- and high-season rates, and as long as they are published there is no resentment. Indeed, I always remember a restaurant customer visiting from New York who was staying in London in January at a famous five-star hotel at a rate of £400 and enjoying it. On asking for the same type of room in April and June he was quoted £1100 and £1800 respectively. 'But I want the same room,' he said to them, but was firmly told that demand dictated the prices. These weren't standard seasonal adjustments, they were prices set by supply and demand. When you take advantage of demand, often you will do so at the expense of loyalty. He went elsewhere.

Let's put that into context and contemplate this happening in restaurants. Imagine you wanted to go to a popular restaurant, say, on both a Monday and a Saturday and on booking the Monday reservation were told that the 'Median Price Index' for that booking was £37.50. And on enquiring what that meant were informed that this related to the price of a sirloin steak on that Monday, and that all menu prices vary accordingly depending on the demand on that day – with the steak price being the guide. For the Saturday reservation you are told that, based on the same principles, the steak price would be £77.50; would you go? I certainly wouldn't. But I think that sadly we are going to start seeing this phenomenon more and more. It has already commenced in the theatre, and I am afraid it is reflective of the schism in society we are experiencing, where attracting the rich is all operators seem to care about. Not only is this counter to all my beliefs, but it is also creating rich ghettos – which has ramifications because, as I have said before, the most interesting of restaurant clients are often the less affluent.

We all want to feel loved, recognised, heard and cared for in life, and it really is incumbent upon hospitality operators to understand these basic needs and know that we ignore them at our peril.

# Ozempic and other weight-loss drugs

The most frequently asked question of restaurateurs now is not so much about the lack of drinking but the lack of eating – and the looming spectre of Ozempic and other similar weight-loss drugs is ever prevalent. While at the time of writing we are feeling the effects of this in the industry, I am confident that the extremes will level and restaurants will find ways to adapt to this change among the clientele. Sadly, I believe that there is a price to pay for easy diet solutions, and as people realise their muscle mass has degenerated into near atrophy and the weight has come back on and the side-effects will be affecting some of the users quite profoundly – how could it not? – the drug will be the province of those who need and benefit from it and not the vainglorious. There is always a price to pay. It is as frightening as with thalidomide, or as in my own personal experience of a drug from the early 1970s, Sylvasun, which had the brilliant result when taken of making the body increase its sun resistance by a boost in vitamin A and calcium carbonate. It worked for just about everyone, but not for me and some others, for whom it had the opposite effect and led to terrible burning that I still bear the legacy of. People realised they needed to apply sun protection and there is no real shortcut, as with Ozempic.

In the meantime, it is easy to spot those using this drug, as they have desultory attempts to eat smaller plates, with many equally turned off alcohol. The result is a reduction of sales against a background of rising food and employment costs. Something has to give, and I am afraid it will be higher prices and less desire to go out.

The restaurant business will need to become more creative and innovative, with dwell times at table, pricing initiatives, menu compositions and reduced staff numbers. As I write, nobody yet quite understands the exact combination of solutions, but as ever I remain positive about our ability to adapt and thrive.

# Part 5: On reflection, lessons learned

# Notes on opening a business

Most importantly, remember that you will never have enough money, time or people. Your projections will be wrong (one way or another), your opening date will either be too soon or too late, and people will not be honest with you about what either they or you are doing. You're likely to be told what people think you want to hear, rather than the truth.

Your plans will have made God laugh. At times it will seem like there is no rhyme nor reason and life just isn't fair – and yet it can all still be a massive success despite that.

If you are planning on being a restaurateur, it is important to shackle yourself to a few rules.

You must not attach too much significance to anything anyone says. Hear the message but don't necessarily allow assertions to tip the rudder in one direction or another.

Praise will often be insincere, but not necessarily so, and it is crucial that when those reviews come in you remember that they are only opinion and not gospel. And when a bad review arrives and the staff pore over it, ridiculing any inaccuracy or ignorance, remind them firmly that those good reviews are just as inaccurate as the bad ones – we just choose not to notice. What is particularly important is that we never allow the good reviews to go to our head nor the bad ones to debilitate or floor us. We must neither be defensive nor arrogant. If someone does say something congratulatory then take the praise – none of that self-deprecatory English deflection.

Paramount is to constantly reassess the decisions you have made and whether you still believe in them – and in what you are doing – even if others counsel otherwise. It is crucial that you show belief in yourself, your concept and your team if you are going to succeed.

Bear in mind that the average observer, client or critic does not know all the things you are painfully aware of. So when they compliment the décor, don't start telling them that it would have been so much better if your idiot investor hadn't insisted on value-engineering the life out of it. If they like it, just thank them, otherwise you are seen to be questioning their judgement and eye. If they then start asking more specifically about the challenges you faced then by all means share – they will feel as if they are insiders – but never dump your troubles on them. We all know how irritating it is if you compliment someone on what they are wearing and you get the response, 'Oh this old thing, it's nothing, I look terrible.'

I tell staff to be careful of flattery as it can lead to our downfall. I still grimace to think of the sadly now deceased Charles Fontaine who had been our chef at Le Caprice from 1982 to 1985. After a while he decided he wanted to open his own place, and he was looking at modest opportunities in South London when I spotted that the original Quality Chophouse lease in Farringdon was available and encouraged him to take it on. Notwithstanding its uncomfortable seating it was so full of character, with its etched windows proclaiming 'Progressive Working Class Caterer' and I felt that he could develop that 'theme'. In the end Charles basically reproduced mostly the favourites from the Le Caprice menu together with a few more appropriate dishes, but most significantly Charles was a terrific cook. I used to say about him, and to him, that he wasn't the best chef in terms of creating menus or leading a team, but if ever I needed someone to cook for my life it would have been him for sure.

There was a lot of interest in the opening. It was a good site and story and the review that was most anticipated was that of Jonathan Meades, who was reigning supreme as restaurant reviewer at *The Times*. He is not only a brilliant writer but a knowledgeable critic too.

Jonathan loved it. He declared that Charles was a genius, that every detail was thought out so carefully and rarely had anyone displayed such perspicacity and insight into restaurateuring. It was significant, for example, that whilst Charles only had one beer on the menu it was exquisitely chosen in a way that only a new titan of the trade could manage. To have Worthington White Shield was the mark of brilliance.

Charles was rightfully thrilled and his success was guaranteed.

But it also eventually ruined him, and that sadly was because he also now believed what Jonathan had stated – that he was a genius – and it all went to his head, just as all the alcohol and drugs that he subsequently ingested as he was embraced as a 'character' at the Groucho Club during its particularly wild times. He spent too much time at the Groucho, at the expense of his business, revelling in the accolades the short term brought, before he gave it all up, moved to Spain, slipped into obscurity and suffered an untimely death. It was too sad and unnecessary, and I am afraid that it laid bare the truism that you can actually have too good a review.

And the truth about that beer? It was chosen after a conversation with the main wine supplier that went along the lines of: Charles: 'You got any beer?' Merchant: 'Only Worthington White Shield I am afraid.' 'Never heard of it. Is it any good?' 'I believe so.' 'Ok, I'll have that.'

Oh, that we could have had such brilliant reviews – indeed, Chris and I didn't always curry favour with the critics, especially in the early days, but I made it a point not to take offence, and in time it was generally recognised that we weren't show ponies only interested in being fashionable and were actually serious restaurateurs, and as time went on we took the trouble to improve and never coast on our reputation. And if a critic loathed us, I saw it as a challenge and I would seek to bring humanity into the relationship with humour and openness; often they would change their opinion. If you allow a detractor or putative enemy to rile you then they achieve 'double indemnity'.

Lessons were learned over the years: Never announce an opening date, do lots of soft openings, whilst being generous, and then suddenly open. NEVER have an opening party unless it is your first restaurant, because otherwise you will find that when you invite 300 you likely will upset the 3,000 that you didn't. Don't concentrate all your attention on the new restaurant, because you must remember to lavish care and attention on the existing ones and, of course, the staff at them – otherwise you will be seen to have 'lost interest' and they will feel abandoned. In some ways it is no different to having children.

Which leads me to a question I was often asked at staff inductions for Corbin & King: 'Which is your favourite of the restaurants?'

This I would respond to by asking in the room as to who has children, and then how many, which if more than one opens the way for me to ask the respondents, 'Which is your favourite?', making the point that I love all my children, am proud of them all and whilst at times there are moments where it might be possible to think I loved one more, as soon as I see the others I realise it isn't. Just as with my 'restaurant children'. They are all very different but it is fundamental that they are all special to me. I did get thrown on one occasion when the chef who had held up his hand as a father told me he had seven.

And when I asked (confidently) whether he had a favourite, he said, 'Definitely – the middle one; no doubt.'

I yelped, 'No – you can't do that!' and he asked why not?

Another of the questions at the inductions is the apposite, 'What advice would you give to anyone opening their own restaurant?' That's simple – keep complete control. Do not be seduced by the promises of riches based on the premise that 'It is better to have a smaller share of something big rather than a big share of something small'. I am afraid I believe the opposite: for anyone embarking on a venture, know that true happiness and gratification is achieved through control of your own destiny.

What I have realised about 'big business' is that often it is Dracula-like in needing the blood of virgins to feed its development. A new arrival in the market, or indeed a centre of excellence, is spotted and targeted because of their innovation, creativity or quality, and the seduction begins.

The predator sees that the target is achieving things far beyond the capability of capital. They want it, need it, whether by way of investment or acquisition, and so the flattery, the courting and enticement all begin. The innovator invariably succumbs and as soon as they are subsumed it is only a matter of the honeymoon period passing before the acquirer is telling their junior partner how it should do things and, consequently, all that potential and innovation is smothered in bureaucracy.

With my new restaurants I have adapted a completely new model whereby each is a separate company, with the commonality of me being the major shareholder in each. I have managed to avoid the need for any corporate investors and therefore am only working with individuals, whom I think of as partners, with one of them being the principal investor. I am happier than I have ever been since the Caprice Holdings days.

# 'I can't give you a good time
unless you want it'

One fundamental misunderstanding about the hospitality industry is that a customer's only obligation is to make the reservation, and from thereon the onus is on the restaurant to provide a good time. And after all, isn't 'the customer always right'?

But this doesn't work. If we approach anything with negativity we are unlikely to extract joy. So my first emphasis for anybody eating out is on that of attitude.

Beyond attitude, here are some tips for the restaurant goer to help them enhance their experience. Several of these also apply to entertaining at home or indeed in a restaurant's private dining room.

## Getting the table in the first place

There is normally quite a disparity between how an 'Englishman' and an 'American' obtain a reservation in a restaurant, and it comes down to using confidence – but avoiding arrogance. The English way is unsurprisingly based on self-deprecation and goes along the lines of:

'Hello, I am sorry to bother you, and I know this is a foolish request, and I am sure you are full, but would you by any chance happen to have a table this evening? You don't? Of course not – silly of me to trouble you.'

Normally fails.

As opposed to the American version: 'Hello, this is "John Smith" and I will be coming this evening at 8.30 – table for two.'

Might succeed.

The best way is to combine the two.

'Hello, this is John Smith and I would be grateful for a table for four tonight at 8.30 p.m. – although I can be flexible and would only need the table for an hour, I can give it back by 9.30, etc.'

The restaurant will appreciate you setting the parameters and is more likely to oblige with this sort of request and will be happy to accommodate. Restaurants you know also prefer to have you identify yourself up front, otherwise there is a dilemma if they turn you down and then you identify yourself afterwards. You can take it further with reservations in terms of the nature of the table. Most restaurants get irritated by specific table requests but will not mind if you say, 'I love your booth tables, should one be free.'

You are already establishing yourself as a regular with an understanding of how it works and are therefore much more attractive to them.

I am writing this from an assumption that we will continue to be able to phone restaurants. In these days of online reservations, I know all too well how hard it can be to track down a phone number for an establishment.

Next is the critical part of restaurant enjoyment – how you seat yourselves. If you are two couples at a square table, sit next to your partner so that you're both facing the other couple. If you're a couple and a solo guest, the same principle applies: couple stays together on one side of the table, solo guest faces both of them. This goes counter to many people's instinct, which is to split the couple and sit the guest between you. Disastrous. The guest/guests are now forced to keep turning from side to side when talking to the couple, whereas if the couple is kept 'together' you can talk to them both without moving your head – just moving the eyes. Have a go and see what I mean. Often, you want to speak to one person more than the other but you don't want the 'other' to feel excluded. Only ever sit either side of a guest if you are negotiating, because whilst one of you holds their attention the other can make signals without them knowing.

The polite host will also often make the mistake of giving the guests the 'good' seats looking out into the restaurant and places themself with their back to the room. This is painful for both the host and the staff. Always choose a seat from where you can communicate with the staff with your eyes, so you can be asked whether you want a new bottle of water or wine with just a discreet presentation answered with a nod – otherwise you will be constantly interrupted or looking over your shoulder.

If, as a host, you want to be sure to pay the bill, do mention this at the beginning of the meal, as any decent restaurant will only give the bill to the person who reserved. If a guest attempts to pay on the sly, the host would normally be told. Do consider whether to be gracious rather than macho, but certainly upbraid any restaurant which accedes to an unofficial request.

## Entertaining at home or in a private room

Setting the scene – table size, lighting, music and timing – are all so important to ensure guests feel welcomed, comfortable and relaxed. Whether you are entertaining at home or in a restaurant's private dining room, you should spend some time getting these elements right.

Food-wise, it is important to remember that there is a tendency for people to eat with their elbows in, and actually passing and sharing the starters is much more fun and gets the elbows out and the interaction and conviviality going. Don't do all courses this way, though – better to have the mains plated and allocated – especially with the more prevalent intolerances and allergies.

If I'm hosting more than eight in a restaurant private dining room, I personally prefer that, having ascertained any dietary needs, everyone eats the same wherever possible, and there's no interference from orders being taken. Nobody expects a choice at your home, so nor should they at a restaurant.

When inviting guests, be very specific about the time that dinner will be served at. There's nothing worse than issuing invitations for 7.30 p.m. and some don't arrive until 8.30. And if you want a dress code, make it very specific – none of this 'dress to impress' or 'smart casual' – be more specific, but ideally have none unless Black Tie.

Don't have people at cocktails before dinner for more than thirty minutes or so (weddings, one hour max). The golden rule these days is that coffee is served by 10.30 p.m. so that the early sleepers can leave without guilt and the carousers can dwell.

Avoid tables that are too large. Whether at home or in a restaurant, table size and shape are fundamental in determining the success of the evening. One of the classic mistakes is to have an oblong table with people sat along either side and no one at each end. So if it's a table of ten, never allow the venue or yourself to seat five a side – always have people at the ends – even if it's a squish. The same applies to round tables: once you get over four people, the amount of space per cover needs to reduce otherwise you are consigned to one of those ghastly wedding table experiences where you can only really hear the people either side of you. Think 1500mm per guest for ten people rather than 1600mm or more, and if on a rectangle allow 500mm per person.

There is also often a mistake made when it comes to placement of a larger group, with the big concern being who sits next to each other. However, this is only really relevant if they are seated at a very large round table or a more formal wide rectangle. Most dining tables these days are quite narrow, so it is actually the person opposite, and those either side of *them*, who you converse with.

Conviviality is the key word for me – I want to create an atmosphere that is warm, welcoming, hospitable, relaxed.

Whilst the table size and shape are crucial, there are other elements that are equally important for creating the right environment – with the acoustics and lighting paramount. There is nothing better than candlelight and, as the late Peter Langan taught me, great lighting is as much about shadow. Think closely about your acoustics before you put on music – there is nothing worse than barely audible music. I find it better to wait until later, turn it up and always go retro – relevant to the demographic.

# A formula for success

I get asked repeatedly what the formula for a successful restaurant is and I frustrate by saying that there is none as such.

'Then what are the ingredients?'

There is no recipe, either, but there are two essential ingredients. And as pens and notepads are readied again I frustrate by saying (as I began this book by saying):

'Heart and soul.'

While thinking about how to define what might give that heart and soul, I received an email from the producer of a podcast that I had appeared on as a guest some time ago. It was Natasha Miller's 'Bitter/ Sweet', a series about how aromas and flavour connect to our deepest emotions.

On listening, I understood that the story I shared encapsulated as well as I knew how to my thoughts on heart and soul. Here is the tale I told of one meal, over thirty years ago, that changed my life.

We get our first view to the left, a brick building with smoke coming from it, and to the right, a converted farmhouse that has tables inside. Outside there are more tables, all of them, of course, unoccupied – apart from one. A woman gets up to greet us, so we introduce ourselves and explain that we've been recommended by our mutual friend.

'Oh, you know Jean Bernard, we love him so. Unfortunately, we are closed today.' But then they look at us and say, 'Why don't you join us?'

So we join the family on their day off. 'We're just having a simple lunch,' they said. We sat down at the end of a wooden table, slid onto a bench, and we were left to get on with ourselves. We were sharing, but we weren't family. They were unintrusive but made us feel welcome.

A litre of rose wine is opened and put before us. And out comes a whole selection of terrines with some bread and I think that's great. That suits me. That's my lunch. That's perfect. I start eating. I don't know quite why, but there was something about the atmosphere – I felt as if I was in a 1970s French film. The Mistral was coming up. The Mistral has this strange effect; it can drive people mad, but it was in its embryonic stage and we were far enough inland that it didn't hit us hard. The leaves were rustling in the wind as it came through and this smoke was being blown over to the restaurant, and there's something special about the smoke.

As I eat, my wife tells me to slow down. 'I think you'll find there'll be more.'

Really? And at that moment a mammoth platter of stuffed mussels comes out of the kitchen. Now, my day-off lunch might at home have been the patés, but suddenly I realised, of course, that the family are cooking for themselves and it's their opportunity to really enjoy their own food. And so the mussels come. And then I think, wow, that was a fantastic lunch.

Until I realised the smoke, too, had a purpose – it smelled so special because they were baking a lamb in the wood-fired oven out in the yard, which was served with flageolet beans on a plate. Soon after a salad came, and with the salad some fresh goat's cheese, which was straight from its making. And at every turn of the way, because I had no expectation, the enjoyment was enhanced. Suddenly everything tasted better. Sounded better. Smelled better. Right through to the coffee, which was then put down in front of us; somehow, even though it had that chicory element to it, as was common in France at that time, it still tasted wonderful.

Curiously, although delicious, I can't remember the lamb as clearly as everything else. I can remember the cheese, which was almost curd, vividly. I can see the mussels on the tray. I think it was the smell of the lamb which impacted on me more than even the taste of it. Every flavour seemed special, even the rosé wine, which was a very, very simple one.

And then the family wouldn't take any money off us. We insisted. Eventually we were allowed to pay, I think it was five francs, which was the equivalent of about 50p at the time. The generosity that came out of that whole experience was probably what profoundly affected me through the rest of my life.

As I ate I reflected on how lucky I was; from an inauspicious start, my life has turned out to be pretty perfect. I've had a lot of very memorable meals, most of which I've forgotten. But my favourite meal was this one in France. That's the meal I always return to.

I learned a lot from the simplicity of it, and I've long held the belief that the best meals aren't necessarily the ones had in the plushest of surroundings. All you need in a restaurant is that you're not cold or hot and that you feel secure – and that can be with a wooden table and a chair. It's the conviviality of other people. It's the conviviality of food. I learned that food is only part of the equation. I think of food as being the catalyst of things to happen.

That's just one of the many lessons I got from it, but ultimately it was the welcome and the generosity, which is a word which I try to carry through everything I do as a restaurateur. Altruism. The idea of doing something for somebody else without expecting any personal gain whatsoever.

Nowadays, people think hospitality is a more perfunctory thing about asking questions, and so on. Actually, it's a generosity of spirit.

*My wife and I were driving in France, near Avignon, because a friend in Paris had told us of his very good friends who had a simple, rustic, country restaurant in the area – we're talking about 1986. With great anticipation we drive into the car park, and at that same moment realise that it's a Monday and, as is often the case with restaurants in rural France, it's closed.*

Listening back to the podcast put me to reflecting on the very nature of enjoyment derived from all the senses. Just as when we clink glasses in a toast in order to employ the sense of sound that completes the set – in that sight, smell, taste and touch are already utilised – it could be said that the complete experience of conviviality needs the same factors.

Whether eating with friends or indeed alone, at home or in a restaurant, the combination of the elements that are stirred into the cake mix of happiness along with the food, décor, staff, fellow guests and atmosphere create the alchemy of heart and soul.

# Afterword

In writing this book, I have been beset by the anxiety of wondering whether I could have done it better, asking myself: Is it enough? What did I leave out? Did I explain myself clearly? Have I done justice to the opportunity?

In truth these questions – and a host of other insecurities – are exactly those that I have been asking over the course of my entire career. They are at the heart of being a restaurateur or entrepreneur, if your aim is to do it properly.

And if you aren't aiming to do it properly, and to execute *everything* in your life to the best possible result, then what is the point? 'Enough' is never enough.

In the angst-ridden state of mind I consigned myself to as a restaurateur, forever cross-examining myself as to whether I have given of my best, I have also been glancing at my shoulder, where André Gide has resided ever since I first heard his aphorism: 'Every man should have three careers.'

And whilst I will always wonder whether I should have pursued a different one, I will take the opportunity to amend that statement to: 'Every man or woman should *enjoy* three careers', because it has to be fun.

If it isn't, please concentrate on changing it. And through striving for excellence, remember to also temper your thoughts with Beckett, rather than looking solely to Gide:

'Ever tried. Ever failed. No matter. Try again. Fail again. Fail better.'

# A life in restaurants, a chronology

## 1973–1976 Charco's Wine Bar, Chelsea

An early pioneer of the wine bar phenomenon of the 1970s. Wine bars came about because of a cartel maintained by all the pubs that prevented the granting of new 'full licences' – only limited wine bar licences. Owned by the caterer to the Royal Family, Searcys, and a sister operation to the larger and more licentious 'The Loose Box' in Knightsbridge (I kid you not about the name). I worked there initially to supplement a meagre merchant banking salary and then switched to full-time while waiting to go up to Cambridge. However, a fateful roll of the dice meant I never got to Varsity.

## 1976–1979 La Grenouille, Battersea

I was persuaded by the French businessman Jan-Michel Gautier to join his burgeoning group, which consisted of a restaurant, wine bar, patisserie and wine importer. Battersea had street cred thanks to the likes of Princess Margaret and Viscount Snowdon. I hated every moment of my time there, but I learned about restaurateuring and wine from every aspect – as well as some of the pragmatic ways a restaurant can stay in control in the face of bad behaviour.

## 1979–1981 Joe Allen, Covent Garden

On the cusp of leaving the hospitality business, I was persuaded not to do so by the brilliant John Maxwell (Max). One of the brightest and most intelligent men I have ever met, Max had a first-class degree from Harvard and was a Rhodes Scholar and yet was happy running the front of house for new arrival from New York – Joe Allen. Under the general manager Richard Polo it was like a speakeasy in feel and attracted all the theatre world and plenty of royalty. It was here that Peter Langan tried to recruit me, and also in these years that I got to know Chris Corbin by visiting Langan's Brasserie – the other 'hottest restaurant in London' at the time.

### 1981–2000 Le Caprice, St James's

My first restaurant – co-owned with Chris Corbin – on the site of the old Caprice, the great post-war haunt for the showbiz, film and fashion worlds, but no longer recognisable as such when we took it over. Initially backed by fashion retailer and designer Joseph Ettedgui, we parted company after only four months. Designed by minimalist Eva Jiřičná for a budget of £30,000. It became the restaurant of the Eighties and was frequented by Diana, Princess of Wales, right through to all the new world of early Eighties pop and punk worlds.

### 1990–2000 The Ivy, Covent Garden

This was the second restaurant in our newly formed 'Caprice Holdings' group, and one I had coveted since first setting my eyes on it in 1977.

Another long-standing London institution (since 1917), in its heyday it had been *the* theatre restaurant, but it had fallen on hard times. Nevertheless, it was difficult to prise it away from the family of the daunting media mogul Lord Grade. Unquestionably London's restaurant of the Nineties, it became like a club due to the frequency of attendance by its regulars. I don't think London will ever see quite the same concentration of celebrity in a restaurant ever again.

## 1998–2000 J. Sheekey, near Leicester Square

A fish restaurant since 1896, J. Sheekey had fallen into disrepute, and most people were shocked when I told them it was on my mind as the perfect sequel to The Ivy. Indeed, it was the antithesis of my own spec as to what our next restaurant should be. David Coffer, the agent, spluttered and swore at me when I asked him to represent us on the acquisition. He repeated back my requirement that he should find us 8,000 square feet, on one floor with one large room, pointing out that, 'Sheekey's is 3,500 square feet on two floors with five rooms!' To which all I could say was, 'Yes, but it feels right.' This is why I encourage everyone to follow their instinct and intuition.

## 1998 Caprice Holdings majority control sold to Luke Johnson and the Belgo Group

Chris and I stayed on until Mr Johnson announced he was going to do a 'management buy-out' in 2000. We decided to leave them to it.

## 2003–2022 The Wolseley, Piccadilly

Despite the magnificent building – created by architect William Curtis Green as the Wolseley Motor Company showroom in 1921 – nobody could believe we would dare to take on the previous failure that was China House on Piccadilly. But the building gave us the opportunity we had been looking for to move from being exponents of brasseries to creating grand cafés. The Wolseley provided the challenge we needed.

## 2006–2009 St Alban, Lower Regent Street

The ill-fated St Alban never quite took off – despite being a favourite for many. We tried to be innovative in both the menu and the décor, but it wasn't widely enough understood, notwithstanding that the Mediterranean-inspired food was probably our best ever. Meanwhile,

we had been looking at an opportunity on the site of the old Theatre Museum in Covent Garden and, having been offered a substantial premium for the St Alban site, we decided to accept. In the end the new site didn't happen because businessman Richard Caring, who had since become chairman of Caprice Holdings, gazumped us at the last moment, even though we had signed the contract. Not the finest hour for the landlord, Capital & Counties.

## 2009–2011 The Monkey Bar, New York

This restaurant came from my longstanding dream to open The Wolseley in New York. This was a challenging period in my life but immensely rewarding in many ways – not least because it occasioned me meeting my wife Lauren.

## 2011–2022 The Delaunay, Aldwych

After the debacle of losing the Theatre Museum, The Delaunay offered a wonderful opportunity to create a restaurant from scratch within the brand-new interior of a traditional building. Very much a kindred operation to The Wolseley but with a greater theatrical following. It is another Grand Café and followed suit on The Wolseley by also being named after a car brand – The Delaunay-Belleville. It was an early example of my pleasure in creating stories about new restaurants – as if they had always been there. In this case I told the story of two Jewish refugee brothers from mid-Europe who started with a café (The Counter) and then based on the success expanded into the space next door, where they established a significant restaurant.

## 2012–2022 Brasserie Zédel, Piccadilly Circus/Soho

I was often offered sites by our agents David Coffer and Tracey Mills that took me seconds to decide on. When Tracey asked, 'Would you be

interested in the old Atlantic Bar & Grill?' my response was, 'Let-me-think-about-it. No!' But she persuaded me to have a look, and it was love at first sight. When I went back to the office to tell Chris and our colleagues, there was an immediate and unanimous resistance. 'Too close to Wolseley, second basement, no light, Piccadilly Circus ghastly' – the list of objections went on. But when I said we were going to emulate Bouillon Chartier in Paris, Chris understood. Big capacity, low pricing, atmospheric, fast and fun. The interior was so glamorous and opulent that we could afford to do so.

Instinct played a part, and when I showed Chris around the spaces all were self-determining: ground floor café, then down to the American cocktail bar and into the brasserie, but when we entered the space at the base of the stairs Chris asked what it was going to be and I didn't as yet know. And then in that moment it came to me and I said 'cabaret', at which he buried his head in his hands. True, it was risky, but it brought another dimension that made the whole place. For two years everyone said I had got it all wrong and the investor was telling me that my 'vanity project' was never going to work.

But Zédel became a massive success and soon exemplified that old saying: 'Success has many parents – Failure is an orphan.'

This was the third restaurant we opened within twelve months. Originally meant to be a Wolseley outpost, I couldn't go through with it; I believed we needed to create a restaurant for Chelsea that felt it belonged there. It was the first full 'story' restaurant – the tale of a French manager run out of a Saint-Germain, Paris, café/brasserie for having seduced the owner's daughter. 'You will never work in Paris again!'

He arrives in London in the late 1920s and gravitates to the then affordable Chelsea and opens a small bar (the room that remains the bar). And having succeeded with serving food as well he then took on the corner room next door and then the third room post-war. If you look carefully all the rooms are decorated with different floors, walls, ceilings, panelling and period photos and posters. (The third room is an homage to French Cinema of the 50s and 60s, and you will find photos of Claudette Colbert who ultimately gave her name.) Colbert was an immediate and gratifying hit.

When looking for a new location, I was beguiled by this space on Marylebone High Street, despite its terrible history of failed restaurants. However, on enquiring, I was disappointed to discover it had already been taken by Bill Granger. Just as I was about to go for another site, I asked the agent to check whether the Granger deal had gone through, and on hearing Bill had withdrawn, I moved quickly. My then-investors tried to force me to open another Colbert, but I had other ideas. The story of the Fischer family escaping Vienna emerged in my imagination, and led to the creation of what could be seen as a typical Viennese restaurant with plenty of influence from a favourite of mine: Zum Schwarzen Kameel.

Yet again I was criticised for not playing safe, but soon Fischer's garnered a very faithful following. Although comparatively small, it was important that this was a restaurant with comfort, authenticity and intimacy, and the inclusion of fourteen corner tables and booths made it a favourite for those who had tired of the large, hard-edged contemporary rooms so much in vogue.

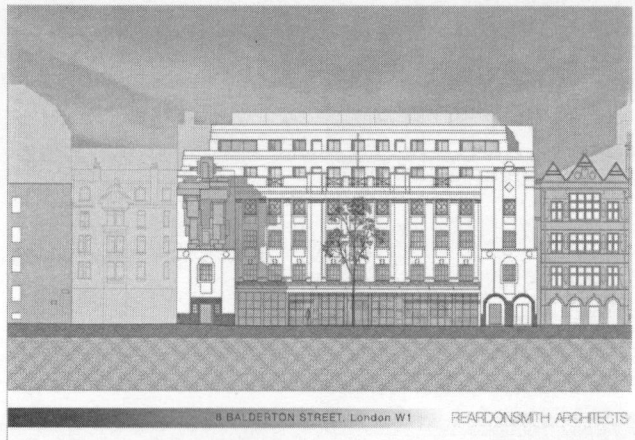

8 BALDERTON STREET, London W1     REARDONSMITH ARCHITECTS

This remains in my mind a tale of injustice, and unusually for me it still occasionally rankles. I had finally found a hotel and won the competition for it, but just then the financial crash of 2008 arrived and my investors disappeared. To cut a long story short, I ended up being forced to do it as a joint venture with the Freeholders Grosvenor and, despite appalling behaviour and cost-cutting by some of their staff (now departed), I really enjoyed creating, designing, building and operating what became an award-winning hotel. This was my most in-depth imagined story, which told the arrival of one Jimmy Beaumont in 1920s London to build a hotel in order to escape Prohibition in New York. Everything was created as if Jimmy had been the proprietor, and all I did was refurbish it to its former glory in a modern idiom. We demolished an Art Deco car park behind the facade and built the hotel from scratch, presented as if it had always been there.

Unfortunately, I got caught in a battle between my private equity investors and the new CEO for Grosvenor, Craig McWilliam, who was trying to make a name for himself by scoring points against old foes. It wasn't going to be a problem because Gerald, Duke of Westminster, had promised me protection and security from the 'ghastly' Craig, but then sadly died three weeks later, and I was doomed. I had to surrender the lease – one of the most distressing experiences of my life. And whilst there was plenty of schadenfreude to be had later, I had much rather not rely on that for recompense.

## 2015–2022 Bellanger, Islington

A promising room, a good position on Islington Green, affluent and mixed neighbourhoods, a dearth of larger restaurants in the area, ground-floor kitchen, external terrace. All portended well and yet somehow it didn't work. I decided that it should be a very authentic Alsatian brasserie (brasseries were the restaurants opened by '*brasseurs*' – brewers – to help sell their beers, and because of the constant fights between France and Germany for the region, many had moved to Paris and other French cities. Hence the tradition of *choucroute* (dressed sauerkraut) and other dishes from the German connection.

We were ready to throw in the towel when we got an offer to sell the lease in 2018. Unfortunately, the deal fell through and we decided to carry on, but still marketing it until we closed in the summer of 2019. Another offer floundered, and because of the ongoing outcry of the closure we then counter-intuitively reopened during the 2020 pandemic and enjoyed reassuring success. Whether it would have been better to have taken an earlier decision to close is up for debate.

## 2019–2022 Soutine, St John's Wood

The timing was unfortunate on this one, in that we went into the pandemic during our first year. Nevertheless, it fulfilled a dream of mine to open in North London. Its story was tied up with the nearby St John's Wood Art School, originally opened on the return of a certain Mr Calderón from teaching in Paris, where he consorted with the likes of Modigliani, Chagall and . . . Soutine. It was full of artistic references and also paid due deference to its proximity to Lord's cricket ground nearby. The restaurant is a paean to the bistros of Paris, and despite the challenges it developed into a popular neighbourhood spot.

## 2022 – Minor take control of all Corbin & King restaurants

The pandemic also served as a catalyst for this rather dramatic change for me. There had been plenty of differences of opinion and the arrival of Covid served to exacerbate the division between the operators and investors since Minor invested at the end of 2017. After a long battle, the only way to resolve the problem was for one side to buy out the other, and it was clear that Minor had a greater appetite for control and duly won an auction for the company by outbidding me and my new backers.

## 2022/3 – the formation of Jeremy King Restaurants

A fascinating time for me, which enforced the belief that my premature retirement was one of the most interesting periods of my life. It gave me time to reflect on the business in a climate that was inordinately hard for most restaurateurs, with staff shortages and rapidly increasing energy costs taking a toll. It was during this 'retirement' that I determined how I would return to work – and how I would be a better restaurateur and the benefits would be felt by customers and staff alike. First, I had to find new projects, and I surprised myself by discovering the initial one in West London.

## 2024 Arlington, St James's

Meanwhile, I was carefully watching the surrender of the lease of Le Caprice by Richard Caring and I was naturally interested – but not if I was going to have to pay a premium. Initially, Le Caprice carried on well enough after Chris and I left in 2000, but it eventually went into decline and, despite a refurb in 2011, it was no longer pre-eminent, particularly in the face of so much more competition. London had established itself as a major player in the international culinary stakes, quickly despatching the reputation for poor food that had endured into the Eighties. By 2020 and the arrival of the pandemic, Le Caprice had rather fizzled out, and it never reopened after lockdown.

Now it had come to market, and although I didn't want to deal with the current tenant, it became clear that the landlord (one of the good ones and unchanged since our tenure) was going to be realistic, so my first port of call was to Jesus Adorno, longstanding maître d'hôtel of Le Caprice, to ask if he was interested. He confirmed he was before I had even asked the question. I had been apprehensive about being seen to be returning to the restaurant scene purely with Le Caprice, but now that I had announced The Park, things were falling into place.

However, it couldn't be called Le Caprice, after my request to Richard Caring to relinquish the name was rejected. Not a problem, I felt, and I quickly established, along with input from customers, that 'Arlington' was the name. It had been trading as 'The Arlington' back before we first acquired the lease in 1981, and it was felt that there was no statement in the name, particularly as we would be recreating the original restaurant interior.

It was a bigger endeavour than most imagined, and I spent a great deal of time and money in making it look as though I hadn't changed anything – in truth, very little of the original decor had remained. The only real sadness was the loss of the original guest washroom interiors from the 1920s. The major reversion, though, was to remove all the misguidedly installed, backlit, white onyx behind the bars and reinstall the mirrors that had made the bar such a popular place to sit. In the end it didn't work out with Jesus, but a wave of nostalgia and the creation of a new audience has made it a great success. I was asked by many whether it was emotional for me to be back where it all started, and I would explain that my true emotion came out when I walked back down those stairs after over twenty years and now it was back to business. But then I saw the emotion in the eyes of those who came through the door – tears even – and I realised what it meant to me.

## 2024 The Park, Bayswater

I was in no hurry to even look at this site, but encouraged by David Coffer I visited and was immediately beguiled by the space, the building itself, and its proximity to Hyde Park on a major thoroughfare. Here was an opportunity to create a Grand Café for the early twenty-first century rather than mimic those of the early twentieth century. It opened in June 2024 and the nature of it evolving was one of the most enjoyable 'concept' processes I have experienced. It soon became clear to me that if I imagined that this restaurant was on Central Park rather than Hyde Park, and that it was being conceived by the likes of Danny Meyer, Jonathan Waxman and Stephen Starr in New York, then its nature would quickly emerge. It has presented me with the opportunity to indulge my love and admiration of the new American cuisine created by the likes of Alice Waters, Jeremiah Tower, Michael McCarty, Larry Forgione (and those already mentioned above) with a European/Californian influence. There is an emphasis on the quality of ingredients; simply cooked and served within the clean lines of a contemporary restaurant, but one that has the mentality of a Grand Café.

## 2025 Simpson's in the Strand

I have held a fascination with Simpson's ever since I first visited it in the 1970s, and even tried to acquire it in 2000 when we sold Caprice Holdings.

Simpson's is one of the last of the grand dame restaurants in London, and in many ways it remains faithful to the 1828 original and 1904 rebuild. Owned by The Savoy Hotel, next door, it quickly established itself in the nineteenth century as not only the home of chess in the UK but in the twentieth century more so for the home of roast beef, which was served in its ground-floor 'Grand Divan' restaurant. It is an extensive property and also has two bars as well as a first-floor banqueting suite and further restaurant that, in less-enlightened times, was known as 'the ladies' restaurant'.

It will be the largest restaurant I have yet to launch.

# Acknowledgements

Ideally I would like to thank my ghostwriter, but typically I was ostensibly headstrong and foolish enough to have declined the offer of using one. That offer came from the estimable publishing editor Louise Haines at 4th Estate. But she cajoled and convinced me that this book would be worth reading even if I wrote it myself, all with the help of long-suffering agent Tim Bates at Peters Fraser and Dunlop, which in turn is patiently and brilliantly headed by my dear friend and mentor Caroline Michel, who is actually completely responsible for me even attempting something I never dreamt I could achieve myself. And thanks to the inspirational EJM who believed in me when I didn't. Of course, the spectre of Ed Victor hovered above me throughout, encouraging and flattering, whilst the positive and kind editing of Ana Fletcher and Alex Gingell bullied me over the finishing line where the already published Keith McNally & Graydon Carter were lying in wait to unwittingly intimidate the hell out of me, along with the Godfather of New York restaurants, Danny Meyer, who 'set the table' for us all.

Of course, my children, Hannah, Margot and Jonah have taught me more than anyone about life, and my wife Lauren has challenged me to look at it all in a different way.

I am grateful to you all.

# Picture credits

p.268  Soutine (Jonathan Wilson / Alamy)

p.269  Arlington (David Loftus)

p.271  The Park (David Loftus)

p.272  Simpson's (Robert Evans / Alamy)

Illustration by Barry Blitt